These Purple Years

Amelia Fielden
These Purple Years

These Purple Years
ISBN 978 1 76041 559 4
Copyright © text Amelia Fielden 2018

First published 2018 by
Ginninderra Press
PO Box 3461 Port Adelaide 5015
www.ginninderrapress.com.au

Contents

Introduction	**9**
Previously Published Work	**11**
Australia	**13**
All You Need Is Love	15
An Appetite for Poetry	16
Bimblebox Art Project	17
Eucalypt: A Tanka Journal	18
Food For Thought	25
Grevillea & Wonga Vine: Australian Tanka of Place	26
Iconic Moon	27
Ink to Paper	28
In Response to Bridges	31
In Response to Persian Music	33
Not Very Quiet	34
100 Tanka by 100 Poets of Australia & New Zealand	35
paper wasp	36
Ps and Qs	37
Pesto Poetry	38
Poetry à la Carte	40
Pour Me a Poem	41
Ragged Edges	43
Tanka To Eat	44
The House is Not Quiet and the World is Not Calm	45
The Melody Lingers On	46
Canada	**47**
Gusts: Contemporary Tanka	49
Magna Poets	60
Many Windows	62
Never-ending Story	63
Poetry That Heals	65

England	**67**
Earth: Our Common Ground	69
Skylark: A Tanka Journal	70
Internet	**99**
100 Gourds	101
Japan	**103**
International Tanka	105
Our Voices on the Winds	109
Pandora	110
Tanka Ōrai	111
International Tanka Festival Competition	110
The Tanka Journal	113
New Zealand	**129**
Downunder Japan	131
Kokako	133
Serbia	**155**
Haiku Novine	157
Osvit	158
USA	**159**
All the Shells	161
Atlas Poetica: A Journal of Place	162
Bright Stars: An Organic Tanka Anthology	186
cattails	193
Caught in the Breeze	195
Fire Pearls: Short Masterpieces of Love and Passion	196
Haibun Today	198
Moonbathing: a journal of women's tanka	202
Poems of the World	204
Portholes: Anthology of Tanka Sunday	205
Ranpu Shimpo	206
red lights	207
Ribbons: Tanka Society of America Journal	219
Ribbons Tanka Café	242

Ripples in the Sand	247
Season's Greetings Letter	248
Storyteller	253
Take Five: Best Contemporary Tanka	255
The Right Touch of Sun	257
United Poets' International World Congress Anthology	258
Wild Voices	259
Previously Unpublished Work	**261**
Solo Tanka Strings	263
Responsive Tanka Strings	278
Tanka Tales	280
Excerpts from Tanka Diaries	286
About the Author	**315**

Introduction

A long while ago, I heard of an old Japanese tradition which associates the colour purple with the seventies, and endorses it as appropriate for wearing by people in that venerable age group. Then, when I turned seventy, I joined the Red Hat Society, founded in the USA in 1997 as 'the place where there is fun over fifty'. This society takes for its motto, so to speak, a poem called 'Warning', by the UK poet Jenny Joseph (1932–). The first verse of 'Warning' begins thus:

> When I am an old woman I shall wear purple
> With a red hat which doesn't go and doesn't suit me.
> And I shall spend my pension on brandy and summer gloves
> And satin sandals, and say we've no money for butter.
> I shall sit down on the pavement when I'm tired
> … And make up for the sobriety of my youth!

A nice synchronicity between East and West, isn't it?

Loving the colour purple, I quite often wear it, not just to Red Hat Society functions.

I was born in 1941, and most of the tanka in this book have been written and published during my 'purple years'.

Enjoy!

Amelia Fielden, 2018

the past seems
a landscape of choices
I ventured
hopefully here and there,
never quite arriving

Previously Published Work

Australia

individual tanka published in the themed Australian anthology *All You Need Is Love*, 2015, edited by Amelia Fielden

sunlight
ripples on the pond
flickers
over stone lanterns –
perhaps I love you still

~ ~ ~ ~

bird etchings
in the pale dawn skies
of winter
weeks and weeks
until your probable return

~ ~ ~ ~

when I grow
too old to travel
my dreams
will take me back to Japan
in cherry blossom time

~ ~ ~ ~

sixty-one years
of cherished friendship
remaining alive
only in my memories
the boy and man you were

                                                  R.I.P. Michael

~ ~ ~ ~

tanka published in *An Appetite for Poetry*, the 2013 anthology of the Watson Poets, edited by Fiona McIlroy

> at Joey's café
> the coffee afternoon
> grinds on, while
> flies laze around the dregs
> of poetry-making

~ ~ ~ ~

> chardonnay
> to unwind the path
> of inspiration
> to sweeten the tempers
> before the homecoming

~ ~ ~ ~

a tanka strand written for the Bimblebox Art Project, 2014, edited by Jill Sampson

Taeniopygia Guttata

zebra finch,
what a big bulky name
for tiny you
who do not gallop striped
across the Serengeti

orange-beaked bird
you flit from bough to bough here,
pursuing your love
with beeps and rhythmic songs
learned from your father

and when you
have wooed a mate, taught chicks
their singing,
may you live out your small life
in the Bimblebox grasslands

individual tanka published in *Eucalypt: A Tanka Journal*, 2011–2016, edited by Beverley George; and 2017, edited by Julie Thorndyke

crushing
a eucalypt leaf
in her fist
this foreign fragrance
the journey's essence

~~~~

all my world sleeps
save for a single bird
a rattling blind
and a mind too aware
of what comes after dawn

~~~~

a duet
of magpies flying low
over eucalypts
hazed by smoky dusk…
five o'clock, midwinter

~~~~

honeyed centres
of crimson grevillea
in full flower
lorikeets swinging
tipsily from the boughs

~~~~

autumn afternoon
a stillness of white clouds
in azure bright
I empty my mind, fill it
with chrysanthemums

~~~~

he indulged me
with the exotic cake
I fancied,
smilingly denying
my stronger desires

~~~~

my ex-husband
calls his new child the name
we had chosen
for our son, whose heart
stopped in my womb

~~~~

Monopoly
with my grandchildren
more fun
more profitable
than playing the stock market

~~~~

uncollected
emptied milkshake glasses
fill quickly
with rainbow lorikeets
in the garden café

~~~~

along the prom
lamplights came on at dusk
went out at dawn –
the simple certainties
of a loved child's world

~~~~

is the wind
still in the willows?
a library
of childhood memories
to lend my grandchildren

~~~~

Auld Lang Syne
always sung with gusto
by the uncle
who flung that 'cup of kindness'
in my grandfather's face

~~~~

kookaburra
lingering on the clothesline,
where are
the visitors from overseas
when you want to show off

~~~~

what shall we do
this anniversary
to celebrate
all the happiness
lying behind us?

~ ~ ~ ~

you have changed
and not for the happier –
autumn's decline
now well-established
a barren winter threatens

~ ~ ~ ~

lone marigold
sinking in a vase,
what happened
to the rest of your bunch
brought to this hospice

~ ~ ~ ~

Friday morning
garbage collection:
a hopefulness
of crows gathering
around kerbside bins

~~~~

another day
of small frustrations
then I find
six gardenia buds
on a sickly bush

~~~~

she binds her braids
with silken ribbons
presses roses
in between poems
plays rugby on Sundays

~~~~

a dawn deer
grazing through the orchard
gone in a flash
this life of appearances
and disappearances

~ ~ ~ ~

all those years
while I waited for love
to return,
the magnolia tree reached
higher, perfuming the stars

~ ~ ~ ~

morning stillness
when sky meets the ocean
in the peace
before all begins again –
alone is not lonely

~ ~ ~ ~

lone gull
flapping round the lake
like me
a little forlorn
so far from the sea

~ ~ ~ ~

individual tanka in the food and drink themed anthology *Food For Thought*, 2011, edited by Amelia Fielden

uni canteen
Tower of Babel
falafel rolls
meat pies, makizushi
with many languages

~ ~ ~ ~

long-life noodles
at home in Tokyo
on New Year's Eve
the deep resonance
of a temple bell

~ ~ ~ ~

lasagne and chips
foreign and familiar
mismatched
at an English pub
with a younger lover

~ ~ ~ ~

individual tanka published in *Grevillea & Wonga Vine: Australian Tanka of Place*, 2011, edited by Beverely George & David Terelinck

suddenly
the morning-glory sky
is menaced
by a crocodile cloud
with dark grey underbelly

~ ~ ~ ~

in drought grass
a flock of cockatoos
pecking pecking,
the majesty of flight
halted by hunger

~ ~ ~ ~

unexpected
wisteria billowing
full and fragrant
over ramshackle walls
October in the suburbs

~ ~ ~ ~

a tanka thread written in response to a photograph, by Margaret Kalms, of the moon over the National Arboretum and published in the School of Music Poets' *Iconic Moon* chapbook, 2015, edited by Hazel Hall

The Moon and I

no moon at all
that night we were kissing
in the garden
a borrowed pearl earring
dropped out and disappeared

just sometimes
the scent of spring grass
and jasmine
sets me wondering who
is embracing you now

never seeking
the moon or the stars
I accept
my sunlit reality,
and yet, and yet…

individual tanka published in *Ink to Paper*, the Limestone Poets' Anthology 2016, edited by Kathy Kituai

just a few leaves
left on the autumn trees
by the lake
how much longer
will we sit together

~ ~ ~ ~

heavy with snow
pine trees mutter and groan
around the golf course
in the rising blizzard
a black dog fetches its stick

~ ~ ~ ~

my children
always polished the silver
for special meals –
the children are gone
the silver I have still

~ ~ ~ ~

in the light
from fireplace flames
his lies flicker
over his charming face…
only my feet stay warm

~ ~ ~ ~

two pieces of tanka prose published in *Ink to Paper*, the Limestone Poets' Anthology 2016

1. In Deep Water

The sea, translucent turquoise, smoothes my hot body. Breast-stroking parallel to the shore of Catalina Island, I am hailed mid-lap by two Americans of a certain age, who are floating around in inflatable chairs. An exchange of pleasantries reveals I'm Australian.

On learning that I've just come from a poetry conference at Long Beach, the husband says, 'We LOVE poetry.'

'Every year on this vacation we have our grandchildren memorise a poem to recite at the end of their stay,' adds the wife. 'What was the conference about?'

'Haiku and tanka poetry.'

'Ah haiku – five seven five syllables.'

'Actually my specialty is tanka.'

>   *treading water*
>   *off pebbly Descanso Beach*
>   *I introduce*
>   *Japanese poetry*
>   *to drifting fans*

2. Wild Freesias

I once lived on a small island in the Mediterranean, where limestone villages clustered around piazzas dominated by ornate churches, all glowing golden in the perennial sunshine. Most of the time the sea was a friendly blue, deep and salty, ideal for swimming. But then the occasional winter storms, when waves leapt high against the cliffs and the battlements of Valletta…

Spring came early with the fragrance of wild freesias emerging from rocky ground everywhere.

Yes, I found much to love there, including my two small daughters, and a good friend's husband.

> *my lover's wife*
> *writes in a Christmas card*
> *forty years on*
> *he died last summer*
> *revisiting Malta*

a tanka sequence published in the School of Music Poets' Occasional Pamplets No. 6, *In Response to Bridges*, edited by Janne Graham

Rattling planks

Sunday drive
in the nineteen fifties
where to go
for incompatible parents
with an only child

the Cotter Dam
far enough from O'Connor
to fill in the day…
picnic aboard, Ford Prefect
judders over the gravel road

STOP!
one way, a narrow bridge
of rattling planks
high above the junction
of two sluggish rivers

in the park
golden poplars shedding
last year's leaves –
ice creams from the kiosk
sweeten one afternoon

blackberries
free for the picking
by the stream
overflow our billycans,
dribble down a little chin

three are joined
in these hours, going home
with pine cones
for the fire, a radio
tuned to Sunday Theatre

~~~~~

and two individual tanka

Coppins Crossing:
picnics and paddling
superseded
by a concrete bridge
and a flow of suvs

~~~~

Harbour Bridge climb
on my sixtieth birthday
a foretaste
of his disaffection –
should have called it quits then

a tanka published in the School of Music Poets: Occasional
Pamphlets No.1, *In Response to Persian Music*

        mint tea poured
        from a beaten silver pot,
        long afternoons
        reclined on leather divans
        we converse in Arabic

published in the online journal *Not Very Quiet*, issue 1, September 2017, a new journal for women's poetry edited by Sandra Renew & Moya Pacey

At Least I Still Remember

there was never
any doubt of love
in my childhood
dahlias grown by dad
vibrant in mum's vases

Empire Day
my father in the garden
lighting fireworks
while I watched, enthralled
behind the kitchen window

bias binding
one of those dread items
clever mother
wielded when teaching
her dull daughter to sew

Grandma
crocheted most beautifully
round the edges
of our linen hankies…
all gone now, every one

too late to know
it was always you
from the start –
still, I can cherish
those Elvis recollections

published in *100 Tanka by 100 Poets of Australia & New Zealand*, 2013, edited by Amelia Fielden & Patricia Prime

       from Europe
       your daytime calling
       my deep night,
       our voices making love
       along the sea bed

            ~~~~

individual tanka published in *paper wasp* journal, 2011, edited by
Jacqui Murray, Duncan Richardson & Katherine Samuelowicz

    the other
    asleep beside me,
    I lie awake
    looking at darkness
    disliking my thoughts

~ ~ ~ ~

    'see you soon'
    those commonplace words
    sometimes
    fill my heart with hope,
    sometimes with despair

~ ~ ~ ~

a tanka thread written for a Ps and Qs poetry reading event held in Queanbeyan, NSW, in 2014

I Remember

by the balcony
above my parents' garden
when I was a child
there grew an unusual tree,
a pointless pomegranate

pointless because
no one cared for the sparse fruit
that tree produced
hard-shelled crimson globes with seeds
we picked at, sucking from pins

yet in the mists
of my pre-Canberra life
pomegranates
shine brightly like their jewels
tiny, sour, unexpected

a tanka thread published in *Pesto Poetry*, the 2015 anthology of the Watson Poets, edited by Fiona McIlroy

A Narrow Corridor

this Saturday
much like any other:
fresh coffee
weekend newspapers
a leisurely walk

magpies swirling
down from bright blue sky
leaves, more leaves
blown over the street
knee-deep, a brown dog stumbles

withdrawing
his hypodermic
the vet asks
do you want her collar –
I can't speak yet

later
with sad fluency
I explain
her stroke and death when
suddenly three are two

how hard it is
to bear another's grief –
the white dog
circles house and garden
searching, searching, searching

gradually
emptying of all I've loved
the future
of unknowable length,
a narrow corridor

a tanka string published in *Poetry à la Carte*, the 2017 anthology of the Watson Poets, edited by Fiona McIlroy

Colouring In

parrots winging
across dawn's stained-glass windows,
kookaburras
in chorus on a gum tree –
breakfast with the birds

spring again
the sports ground grasses
dappling
with bright yellow daisies –
no kids to pick them with me

orange
once his favourite colour,
pink was hers –
now they're teenaged goths
in unrelenting black

seldom opening
my drawer of silver spoons,
seldom seeing
all the family gathered
around this old table

colouring in
my greyed seventies
purple, red, green
the way I used to
crayon within the lines

a tanka thread published in *Pour Me a Poem*, the 2014 anthology of the Watson Poets, edited by Fiona McIlroy

The Winter of Discontent

small and white
wild water lilies shine
star-like
in the billabong's dark skies –
will we keep on walking

in the dazzle
from silvering waters
I see clearly
what I want and why
you will not provide it

these vacant hours
in the long afternoons
how I miss
my old life, of never having
enough time…

the complacency
of convenience –
every evening
we sit apart together
in the heated TV room

lots of places
I'll never get to now –
nightly
I meet that same woman
out dog-walking late

are we there yet,
the point of no return?
journeying
from queen-sized to twin beds
then separate rooms for sleep

fractured
into a thousand pieces
this jigsaw life
a puzzle beyond reframing
as a pretty picture

individual tanka published in *Ragged Edges*, Anthology of the Limestone Poets, 2013, edited by Kathy Kituai

       waves swooshing
       in the ocean pool
       I float
       forever freed
       from the need for speech

          ~ ~ ~ ~

       in the reeds
       a red-winged blackbird sings
       for its mate –
       so little response from you
       to my emails

          ~ ~ ~ ~

       filling the tub
       she adds fragrant salts
       hums an old tune –
       such pleasure to stretch out
       alone in bath and bed

          ~ ~ ~ ~

a tanka written by Amelia with commentary by Noriko Tanaka
published in *Tanka To Eat: Themed Tanka Masterpieces by Modern Poets*, 2014, selected by Noriko Tanaka, translated by Amelia Fielden and Saeko Ogi

> crouching to pick
> in the strawberry patch
> my knees tell me
> I have relished the tastes
> of many summers

Strawberries produce fruit on plants low to the ground. That's why to harvest strawberries, one must bend down; after a long while in the crouched position, one's knees are inevitably hurting. It seems that the poet gets sore knees from strawberry picking. She also says that the pain in her knees makes her remember many summers of strawberries. This isn't simply a complaint about the pain : there are sweet memories amidst the soreness, intoxicating memories – all sorts of memories conjured up by her aching knees. The tanka as a whole seems symbolic of the efforts one makes in life.

commentary by Noriko Tanaka
translated by Amelia

previously published individual tanka printed under the heading of 'Three Tanka' in the 2015 anthology of work by Canberra poets entitled *The House is Not Quiet and the World is Not Calm*, edited by Kit Kelen and Geoff Page

>all those years
>walking off the plane
>into Dad's arms –
>will the wagtails still bathe
>in his garden at dusk

>~ ~ ~ ~

>still empty
>my black lacquer box
>awaiting
>something too precious
>to lie uncovered

>~ ~ ~ ~

>we made love
>thirty years ago,
>a few times…
>he still expects me
>to recognise his voice

>~ ~ ~ ~

individual tanka published in the music-themed Australian anthology *The Melody Lingers On*, 2012, edited by Amelia Fielden

on one long note
a cricket serenades
the sultry dark
and all the lovers
of this summer's night

~ ~ ~ ~

casting his net
with those first haunting bars
the clarinettist
hauls me up to the stars:
Midnight in Paris

~ ~ ~ ~

I'd like to think
there is a heaven
where Joan
and Luciano sing,
Margot and Rudolf dance

~ ~ ~ ~

Canada

individual tanka published in *Gusts: Contemporary Tanka*, Journal of the Tanka Canada Society, 2010–2015, edited by Kozue Uzawa

behind low cloud
the sun is a white moon
'night and day
you are the one',
an old song, can it be true

~~~~

winter poplars
pointing like shaved pencils
at ice-blue sky –
deep in my heart, darling
I hold the warmth of you

~~~~

so much love
dancing the parquet floor
on Sundays
when the jazz band plays
at the seniors' village

~~~~

you are dead
and the sun is still shining
children laughing,
but nothing will shift
this boulder on my chest

~ ~ ~ ~

so tranquil here
and yet the thundering
of the ocean
in perpetual motion
beyond our composure

~ ~ ~ ~

the bald eagle
snatches a young crow –
how to justify
survival of the fittest
to my watching grandchild

~ ~ ~ ~

a long life
many 'right' decisions, yet
right for whom?
again the lake churns
with white-capped waves

~~~~

the man
I wanted as my lover
tells me
I am his 'diamond friend' –
these years of acceptance

~~~~

Sunday morning
by an inner city wall
two blankets
neatly folded, two bottles
half full – and that was all

~~~~

a seahorse cloud
gliding through blue, lighter
than the ocean –
in just twenty minutes
my world turned upside down

~~~~

rusted
with recollection
his mind
hard to start now
motors ever more slowly

~~~~

this year I find
wine-coloured hyacinths
without you
at the floral festival
fresh scents and stale memories

~~~~

in the lift
I admire her armful
of red roses –
not right for a funeral
she says, but he loved them so

~~~~

clouds clearing
silver streaks on the sea,
this long long beach –
is seventy-one too old
to be ambitious

~~~~

two careers
three dogs, five children…
those were the days
when the clocks panted
to keep up with us

~~~~

Shakespeare and
nineteenth-century poems
learned by heart –
no wonder there was no space
for physics and algebra

~~~~

ice-blue satin
with a black lace bodice –
twenty-one
her hopes as brilliant
as her homemade ball gown

~~~~

suitcase smashed
she stands at the carousel
wondering
what kind of welcome waits
beyond those exit doors

~~~~

a crow
huddled on a park bench
in thick mist
this lake is an ocean
without horizon

~~~~

spring is blooming
all around, then the call
comes:
our daughter has suffered
another miscarriage

~~~~

my first time
pushing a grown woman
in a wheelchair…
pausing for breath at the pond
I absorb the water lilies

~~~~

calling a friend
widowed this past year,
I'm startled
by her husband's voice
'please leave your message now'

~~~~

such a plain street
suddenly brightened
by the pink blooms
of two crepe myrtle trees –
why not be optimistic

~~~~

sailing along
black swan parents, brown cygnet
between them
the peace and the perils
of an only child

~~~~

caring for you
taking care of you
being careful –
none of that can defeat
the demon dementia

~~~~

old-fashioned love
in sickness and in health
yet
another life beckons
beyond his complaints

~~~~

vanishing
amidst a morass
of worries,
quiet mindfulness –
weeds sprout in our garden

~ ~ ~ ~

spring-blue sky
striped with white contrails…
floating up
from the dental chair
on a draft of ether

~ ~ ~ ~

intently
the caterpillar climbs
a thread
invisible yet strong
like your support for me

~~~~

my stepmother
is turning ninety-two –
as a gift
for her birthday I'll send
a long-lasting orchid plant

~~~~

every day
is greeted with eagerness –
small white dog
your presence in our lives
far exceeds your size

~~~~

individual tanka published in *Magna Poets: taking over the world one poem at a time*, 2011–2012, edited by Aurora Antonovic

remembering you
flying down the hockey field,
remembering me
jiving the night away,
we watch our grandkids play

~ ~ ~ ~

their old dog dies
and then her husband –
'easy to train
this new puppy,' she says
when we meet in the park

~ ~ ~ ~

long twilights
star-brilliant short nights
together…
she thought she loved him
he knew he loved her

~ ~ ~ ~

is regret
really more interesting
then happiness?
so many tanka sing
such melancholy songs

~ ~ ~ ~

'think of me
when you wear this haori'
he whispered
draping the silk around me –
I do, oh I do

~~~~

white daisies
in a green pottery vase
how ordinary
how precious they are,
these gifts from you

~~~~

resting my dreams
on a soft bed-pillow,
I rise
to perform whatever
hard tasks this day demands

~~~~

bodysurfing
my frustrations fragment
then vanish
with waves fanning out
into the calm shallows

~~~~

individual tanka published in *Many Windows: a collection of poetry in all forms, exploring the topic of epiphanies*, Magna Poets Anthology series 4, 2011 edited by Aurora Antonovic

in the roar
of this waterfall
I am deaf
to all past voices –
there is now only you

~ ~ ~ ~

making love
suddenly I wonder
how will I die?
so many times for love
only one time for death

~ ~ ~ ~

the red fog
of an anger suppressed
until
arteries block
and angels descend

individual tanka* published in 2016 on his blog Never-ending Story and translated into Mandarin Chinese by Chen-ou Liu

halving fruit
my second husband's
way of love –
hard to change habits
so late in life

~ ~ ~ ~

I am held
in this bed in this life
by your hands –
where would I be now
if I had said 'no'

~ ~ ~ ~

those wild violets
you'd nurtured for me
bloomed brilliantly
in the early spring
our friendship died

~ ~ ~ ~

* previous publication: 'halving fruit', 2nd place, Tanka Society of America Contest 2000; 'I am held', *Short Songs*, 2003; 'those wild violets', Certificate of Merit, The Japan Tanka Poets' Society Competition for the 7th International Tanka Festival, 2012

individual tanka* published in 2017 on Never-ending Story

bird etchings
in the pale dawn skies
of winter
weeks and weeks
until your probable return

~ ~ ~ ~

shall I sweep
the courtyard again,
will you come
before my summer ends?
the crimson rose still blooms

~ ~ ~ ~

that silver glow
of cherry blossoms
at twilight
poem after poem
opening in my heart

~ ~ ~ ~

* previous publication: 'bird etchings', *All You Need Is Love*, 2015; 'shall I sweep' and 'that silver glow', *Light on Water*, 2010

individual tanka quoted in the book *Poetry That Heals*, 2014, by Naomi Beth Wakan

>too young
>to really be in love
>now too old
>to stay awake all night –
>where did the between go

~~~~

>seniors' outing:
>becoming aware now
>I've entered
>the zone where death parts
>more often than divorce

~~~~

>'mum, don't you
>recognise my voice
>any more' –
>I blame the connection
>but the truth is worse

~~~~

how I wish
my tanka of passion
did not erupt
solely from old memories…
last night's storm is over

~ ~ ~ ~

the years pass
as I yearn to fly free
love holds me still –
yachts moored near the pier
move just a little

~ ~ ~ ~

hilly paths
I walk now where
once I ran…
sometimes the past
must be enough

~ ~ ~ ~

England

a tanka published in the anthology *Earth: Our Common Ground*, 2017, edited by Claire Everett

>   on the bank
>   by the sun-spangled river
>   I am immersed
>   in the smell of water,
>   In the fast flow of time

individual tanka published in *Skylark: A Tanka Journal*, summer 2013, edited by Claire Everett

> dawn would be sad
> if it weren't for the birds
> singing me awake
> another dreary day
> if it weren't for the birds

~~~~

> unprecedented
> this profusion of flowers –
> callistemon
> are you blooming
> to persuade me to stay

~~~~

a tanka sequence written in commemoration of the International Tanka Concert held in Nara, Japan, 19 May 2013, published in *Skylark*, winter 2013

A Long Way From Home

in my porthole
clouds piling on clouds –
somewhere beyond
are the lofty turrets
of Osaka castle

breakfasting here
an ancient pagoda
within sight,
I am blissfully
a long way from home

choice no choice –
were I to live again
in Japan
Nara would satisfy
most of my desires

luminous balls
of bilingual tanka
tossed from the stage,
caught by an audience
of poetry lovers

canopied
with the brilliant green
of young leaves,
the old capital's park
waits for cicada summer

the plane lifts
and already I'm back there
in the land
of responsibility,
checking my diary

individual tanka published in *Skylark*, summer 2014

over the roofs
the dull suburban roofs,
pale purple clouds
of jacaranda float
and catch my useless dreams

~ ~ ~ ~

celebrating
the wisdom of graceful age
with morning tea
in the college gardens,
golden graduates

~ ~ ~ ~

not for nine years
have the wild lilies bloomed
in such profusion –
that was the end of one life,
is this the end of another

~ ~ ~ ~

individual tanka published in *Skylark*, winter 2014

a Facebook photo
of her first solo cake –
this longing
for my granddaughter
to cook in my kitchen

~ ~ ~ ~

forget his words
focus on the iris
in the temple pond
purple and white silence
a zen koan

~ ~ ~ ~

somewhere
in the long dewy grass
a cricket
is chirruping, constantly
I wish I still loved you

~ ~ ~ ~

a responsive tanka string written with *Genie Nakano* (USA) and published in *Skylark*, summer 2015

Fluttering Gold

zen garden
crammed with solemn tourists
photographing
the first few crimson leaves
on a small maple tree

October
leaves crunching under my feet
the bite
of a first red apple…
the day you died

across the world
spring flowers in bloom
at Halloween
kids trick or treating
on a bright mild night

oh, the wind…
the wind is what sets us free
on dark autumn nights
spirits fill the air
swirled with Van Gogh stars

sunflowers
ablaze in their frame
at the Gallery
and in my memory
of last summer's hot fields

all the tanka
we wrote together
memorised
we're here now to sing them
as gingko flutter gold

a responsive tanka string written with *Jan Foster* (Australia) and published in *Skylark*, summer 2015

Free Wheeling

yellow
not my favourite colour
and yet
who would want a world
without sunflowers or wattle

entranced, I watch
tiny honey-eater chicks
dip and dart
among the flax spikes
I almost dug out last week

my chic friend
a French sophisticate,
confides
her greatest pleasure is
hard labour in the garden

in my dream
you whispered a secret
sadly
now I'm awake
I can't recall what it was

with only one
remembering shared events
how lonely
this marriage has become –
time to deadhead our roses

sitting in sunlight
I let my mind drift
free-wheeling
a single heron
cruises a thermal

brolgas dance
through his mystic landscapes
the artist
Sydney Long releases
my mind from the mundane

waltzing together
our rhythm is flawless –
a pity
we step on each other's toes
in our daily life

riding the storm
a cockatoo keeps faith
with its branch
of a huge eucalypt
that wildly dips and sways

the air softens
winter unclenches its fist
as life stirs
hope raises its head
… I search out my passport

a responsive tanka string written with *Giselle Maya* (France) and published in *Skylark*, summer 2015

Welcomed

chirashi sushi
with sweet black and white beans
fastidiously served –
oh for those days and nights
Arashiyama moonrise

first dream
of the New Year,
alone
on a curved bridge, waiting
for my old professor

blown together
by random breezes
blue feathers
and an autumn waka
in my wooden skiff

in the distance
mountains appearing
disappearing…
reality and illusion
jostle in my memory

visiting
potters in Bizen
at o-shōgatsu
we are invited to help
pound and roast mochi

more than the scents
of traditional Japan
it is the tastes
I long for, breakfasts
with white rice and miso soup

high above Kyoto
in a remote hamlet
the artist Akeji
boils plants, berries and bark
to make dye for washi

calligraphy class
copying the kanji
'yuki', snow,
on white paper imprinted
with plum blossoms

after tea lessons
I go to a Kannon temple
praying
my knees may hold out
for the month-long course

bronze vases
of small chrysanthemums
on Buddhist altars –
seasonal flowers always
for home ikebana

Kyūshū –
just arrived by shinkansen
I am welcomed
by a host of violets,
a bowl of green macha

a solo tanka sequence published in *Skylark*, autumn 2015

Last Spring

greening paddocks
patchworked with white lambs
thirty minutes
from suburban streets
to Tulip Tops

through an archway
of pink crab apple trees,
across the bridge
to a small waterfall
splashing down bluebell slopes

bordered
by bright quince blossoms
the stream water
a drifting mosaic
of breeze-blown petals

we stroll on
between beds and beds of tulips:
flame colours,
deepest purple, almost black,
delicate skin tones…

preschoolers
under clustered crimson
double peach blooms,
fidgeting into poses
for group photographs

warm air now
with the fragrance of flowers
an old friend
comes from afar to visit
consoling the past

individual tanka published in *Skylark*, winter 2015

glowing purple
morning glory flowers
with abandon
an only child skips
along the empty lane

~ ~ ~ ~

emotional
independence, counsels
my psychologist –
a skylark rises
flying towards the sun

~ ~ ~ ~

and in 2017

three-thirty
pelican feeding time
at The Entrance
holiday makers hurry
past the refugee tent

a responsive tanka string written with *Jan Foster* (Australia) and published in *Skylark*, winter 2015/2016

Winter Games

six o'clock
in the frosty dark
my three dogs
are ready to start
another day of play

ice hockey match
fiercely contested
…a miracle
heat between supporters
doesn't melt the ice

hot chocolate
topped with marshmallows
and sweet kisses –
all those teen afternoons
of boyfriends' footy games

enjoying
solitaire by the fire
this silence
much more peaceful
since you left

defeated
by my thousand piece jigsaw,
the grandkids
suggest we play golf
on their new e-device

cabin fever –
an explosion of children
outdoors
a snowball fight
better than fists

I remember
icicles hung under
the Eiffel Tower,
forget why we argued
until we departed

in the car park
tussling over a corn chip
two baby sparrows
their fiery exchange
undeterred by frigid winds

cross country run
slowed to a dogged jog
by head winds
straight from Antarctica –
those were the bad old days

missing skier
with night approaching
as we wait
the radio crackles
– they've found him

a solo tanka sequence published in *Skylark*, summer 2016

Equinox

if tomorrow
day is longer than night,
will I
accomplish more, or less –
spring weeds grow and grow

if tomorrow
day is longer than night,
will we walk
all the way round the lake –
magpies are still swooping

if tomorrow
day is longer than night
will we
make time to talk truth –
winds from the Antarctic

if tomorrow
day is longer than night
how many dreams
might colour my sleep –
more dire news from abroad

if tomorrow
day is longer than night
should we admit
past pleasures are past –
blossoms yield now to leaves

a responsive tanka string written with *Kath Abela Wilson* and published in *Skylark*, summer 2016

Back and Forth

summer garden
garden of poets listening
to lyrics
caress the opened roses
tune the green-leafed breeze

cross country and ocean
poets flock to turn
virtual to actual
short songs in the same garden
for a few moments

precious moments
when time seems to stop
before the clocks
start panting again
to keep up with us

flying by
memories they say will flash
before our eyes –
in dreamtime I keep words
from escaping

'to sleep, to dream'…
I ride a ferris wheel
eyes wide open
to the clear-cut scenery
to my dubious future

back and forth
the lilting swing
of a cable car
up and down the mountain
as we compose ourselves

a tanka tale published in *Skylark*, winter 2016

Still the Music

The Nursing Home program for Saturdays and Sundays shows only 'family visits'.

No other form of entertainment.

Not far to drive. But it's like moving into a different world.

>*dawning bright*
>*the day turns to dismal rain –*
>*a faint light*
>*that flickered, now gone*
>*from his old blue eyes*

Too wet to walk in the courtyard today.

I think he still knows who I am, but he neither speaks my name, nor shows any sign of affection for me.

He's losing his words.

I put one of his favourite CDs on the player. And then another.

We sit in the music until an aide collects my husband for five o'clock dinner.

>*whether to keep*
>*battering these fragile wings*
>*against*
>*his fading warmth, or*
>*to fold myself away*

a tanka tale published in *Skylark*, spring 2017

Missing

The little white dog is not taken to The Other Place these days. She does not understand. Because she was such a good girl, they always told her: sitting still during the car drive there; running along the corridors, always finding the door to Dad's room by herself; then doing whatever he felt like…a stroll in the garden, a cuddle at his knees, or just lying quietly while they listened to music.

She does not understand why no more visits. Dad's not at home, so he must be in The Other Place. Maybe he doesn't love her now. Last time she went there he was lying in bed. She jumped straight up to give him a kiss, but he pushed her away. She tried again and Mum said 'stay down!'

Maybe it was bad to jump on his bed.

The little white dog wishes they would give her another chance.

She misses her Dad.

> *heeling now*
> *to dementia,*
> *must she forget*
> *those old family ways*
> *of fun and affection?*

a solo tanka sequence published in *Skylark*, winter 2017

Another Birthday

one dog and I
share the park with eight
corellas
rising to fly their light
through the mists of my mind

purple blooms
of wild morning glory
colonising
a banana palm –
how I love hybrids

creamy crests
on ultramarine waves
I swim
endless love for the sea
today, my birthday

contemplating
a vessel's broad wake
rather than
steering it through the reefs –
those irresponsible years

in the twilight
white clouds of cockatoos
swirling
towards the Norfolk pines –
we say goodbye again

'no moon at all'
played on a harmonica
somewhere
in this dark still night
of many memories

a responsive tanka string written with *Jan Foster* (Australia) and published in *Skylark*, autumn/winter 2017

Twilight Time

a weed struggles
through the cleft in a rock
somehow
I manage to face
yet another day

lavender blooms
all along the garden paths
at the nursing home
he asks 'what's that?' again
and again and again

the road ahead
through mountains and valleys
looping, twisting,
my destination altered
by every challenge met

looking back
with pleasure at the wealth
of journeys
experienced together,
I set my own new course

twilight finds me
sipping a fresh coffee
in the company
of treasured spirits
past, present and future

a tanka tale published in *Skylark*, winter 2017

Hanafubuki: A Flurry of Flowers

blossom petals
swirling in April breezes
translucent white
heavier than snow
lighter that flowers

When my plane lands at Narita it's chilly and raining solidly. Four years since I've seen Nariko. Not so long in the context of 53 years' friendship. But now we are both over 75, it feels too long. From my hotel I call to arrange our meeting. She frets that rain will have damaged the blossoms.

Next morning the stroll to a breakfast café past a diminutive park.

surrounded
by high-rise buildings
four cherry trees
blooming in their own rhythm
under clearing skies

Down the hill, outside the enormity of Shibuya station under reconstruction, I come to Hachiko Square

through the square
past the fire station
up the hill
to home, just yesterday
pushing my child's pram

The statute of 'faithful dog Hachiko' has been a popular rendezvous for more than half a century. Today there is an orderly line of people, Japanese and foreigners, waiting to have photos taken with the bronze dog beneath a canopy of pale flowered branches.

Now I see Nariko approaching through the shifting crowds.

> *a light wind*
> *blows falling blossoms*
> *onto her hair*
> *once like black lacquer,*
> *now streaked with silver*

We bow 'o-hisashi buri desu. It has been so long'.

Twenty minutes by train to our favourite place, Asakusa, where the 'hanami'* season is coming to an end.

> *branches skim*
> *a somnolent canal*
> *casting*
> *petals upon petals –*
> *on the bank sit two painters*
>
> *mandarin ducks*
> *side by side gliding*
> *pink-cloaked waters –*
> *not so simple to achieve*
> *this serenity*

* 'hanami' means 'cherry blossom viewing'

individual tanka published in *Skylark*, summer 2018

the haloed glow
from a street light outside
turns night
into a preview of dawn
for these unlikely lovers

~ ~ ~ ~

new draughts
and old dreams, drifting
through rooms
almost emptied now –
who will buy this pre-loved house

Internet

individual tanka published in *100 Gourds*, 2012–2013, tanka editor Susan Constable

'love
oh love, careless love…'
they've gone again
and I am left sweeping
the sad autumn leaves

~ ~ ~ ~

quiet carriage
only old-fashioned sounds
permitted
the turning of book pages
the rustling of newspapers

~ ~ ~ ~

four seagulls
walking their shadows
along the shore
I once ran easily –
ah, the sands of time

~ ~ ~ ~

Japan

a tanka string published in *International Tanka*, 2017, edited by Mari Konno

After Many Years

magnolias
pink and plump in full bud
against the blue –
slumped in a wheelchair, my love
will not lift up his eyes

am I lost
in the life of a husband
who is losing
almost everything he knew?
few leaves fall from eucalypts

weeks and months
sliding by…slowly
he declines,
quality of life nil
heartbeat relentless

dead-heading
the last summer roses,
I see a blue wren
fly into my courtyard –
alone is not lonely

many years
performing a marriage,
I now rehearse
the role of old widow
for a smaller audience

two tanka tales published in *International Tanka*, 2017, edited by Aya Yukhi

The Study of Ancient History

Over sixty years ago we sat close to each other in the same classrooms, learning the same lessons, the three of us. We can still recite the six declensions drilled into us by Mr. Collier, our golden-haired Latin master.

Now, on a bright winter's afternoon, amid the scents of dampened earth and leaf mould, we are strolling together through Sydney's Botanic Gardens for the first time. Strolling not because of infirmity, but to concentrate on conversation rather than on our pace along the dirt paths.

Stepping over giant Morton Bay Fig Tree (*ficus macrophylla*) roots, I reminisce about my dad bringing me here by tram, so many Sundays when I was a child and he was young and carless.

'These gardens must be special for you,' Katy comments.

I nod, thinking special place, special people

> *out the south gate*
> *past the same old gallery,*
> *cathedral ahead,*
> *still the sun shines*
> *and still we are friends*

Small Flowers

our old dog died
ten days after my husband…
'they will be
companions in Heaven,'
says a friend who believes

For over fifty years I have been checking the box 'married', scarcely noticing that other option, 'widow'.

'widow'? A term sometimes accompanied by words such as 'heart-broken', 'black clad', or 'frail'.

I am none of those. But I am a widow now, and I am grieving for the many good years we had together, and for the years of comfortable old age we shall not share.

asked to name
our favourite flowers
I answer
'small ones, with sweet scents'…
now, where to bury his ashes

a tanka string published in *International Tanka*, 2018, edited by Mari Konno

A Kind of Homecoming

sunset glow
over snow-covered craters…
Mt Rainier
to the right of the plane
I'm almost home again

the surprise
of a camellia hedge
blooming in pink
below clear winter skies
the post person greets me

from grandson's fingers
flow the notes of Chopin's waltz
dancing
past misted windows…
love in the afternoon*

black and white dog
prancing through thick drifts
under grey clouds
a northern December
sketched in my diary

snow melting
from rooftops still outlined
in coloured lights –
you Ghosts of Christmas Past
be gone! now is beautiful

* title of a 1960s film in which Audrey Hepburn is a cello student

a tanka string published in *Our Voices on the Winds*, 2014, Anthology of the United Poets' Laureate International, 23rd World Congress of Poets, Osaka, 2014, edited by Noriko Mizusaki

Tanka Vignettes: Seattle Summer 2013

sun-warmed circuit
cyclists, walkers, runners
round Green Lake
under the azure sky –
are those hawks, way up high

blue dragonflies
skimming bright dappled water,
silver seaplanes
ascending through cloud wisps –
the lightness of summer

seagulls in the air
children in the fountain
simple pleasures
on a north-west afternoon
no sense of time a'wasting

in the lake park
dusk is streaked with orange:
a frisbee
wide-winged butterflies
wandering birthday balloons

how come this breeze
in a Seattle suburb
reminds me
of my seaside Coogee?
must be the love in the air

Pandora: The Bilingual Anthology of Contemporary Japanese & International Poems: in English & Japanese Languages, 2016, edited by Noriko Mizusaki

> a boy
> with his dad fishing
> off the pier
> seagulls circling through blue
> …this timelessness

~ ~ ~ ~

> gleaming
> in his eyes the ice
> of his voice –
> this one of all others
> I thought admired me

~ ~ ~ ~

a tanka string published (in Japanese) in *Tanka Ōrai* journal, August 2015, special edition *Summer in Japan, Summer Overseas*

Summer Downunder

such bright light
early on summer mornings
at the coast
promises long salty days
of unstructured leisure

a sunburned kid
sitting on Santa's knee
requests
a surfboard for Christmas –
festive shoppers throng the mall

holiday time
at the rock pool little girls
in fluoro suits
jumping squealing splashing –
a white flash of seagulls

deep blue harbour –
the old men of the sea
start boat motors,
cast fishing lines, swim out
against the turning tide

the tanka which was judged as 'excellent' in 2013 in the 7th International Tanka Festival Competition of the Japan Tanka Poets' Society

> those wild violets
> you'd nurtured for me
> bloomed brilliantly
> in the early spring
> our friendship died

the tanka which was awarded a Certificate of Merit in 2016 in the 8th International Tanka Festival Competition of the Japan Tanka Poets' Society

> floating dead
> on the pristine fountain
> a grasshopper
> such a small thing
> and yet…

eight tanka strings published in *The Tanka Journal*, 2011–2017, edited by Aya Yuhki

1. Rest In Peace: Kawano Yūko (1946–2010)

2000
    I wanted
    to say how much I
    admired her,
    but we parted there
    still talking of plum jam

2003
    husky-voiced
    fanning her flushed face
    the poet speaks –
    my pen transforms her tanka
    for English posterity

2005
    fluttering
    her blue Kyoto fan
    she glances
    round the respectful room,
    sighs a sensei's sigh

2010
    soon they will bloom
    white, pink, mauve, crimson –
    the poet is gone
    never to return home
    to her cosmos garden

2011
    Nagatani –
    my eager mind, my fond heart
    no longer seek
    the way to the house
    by the bamboo grove

2. In Surfers Paradise, Queensland

sing again
silver-voiced cricket
it's so dark
the birds are sleeping still
sing to me, sing to me

no light reflects
in the river muddied
by recent storms –
how I wish you would
swim away from your grudges

the ibis here
non-sacred scavengers
graceful in flight
grimy and ragged
picking over garbage

remembering
Yūko, how she loved
small wild things,
I consider the weeds
flowering in a car park

at the market
subtropical saplings and
tie-dyed T-shirts
swaying in the breezes
of our years in Paradise

3. April Jottings In Seattle

coming too late
for the crimsons and pinks,
I'm dazzled
by apple-blossom white,
the sheen of young green leaves

in the food court
a friend flourishes
silver chopsticks
for her personal use –
disposables will do me

ferry crossing:
water, islands, sky
grey layers
on this drizzly day
we meet and warm each other

I shelter the boy
under my umbrella,
holding his hand –
so much rain ahead for him
after I'm gone

that young man
sitting against a spring elm –
are his desires
drifting with the clouds, or
rooted like the tree?

they sent me
the obituary, yet
behind my eyes
I'll be seeing you again
in all our special places

4. Vacation On the Big Island

in the queue
at security checking
a young man
with flamboyant flowers
and a diffident smile

blue Hawaii
pool fringed with plumeria
floating
the occasional flower –
no clouds in my sky, for now

palm tree fans
to and fro in humid air
high above
the crimson hibiscus hedge,
a sudden flutter of sparrows

across the sea
the mountains of Maui
rimmed with fire
in the rose-gold sunset
behind the darkening palms

this twilight
a tropical cliché
as I recline
iced Mai Tai to hand,
beside the sighing waves

5. All Above Is Azure Bright

today's dawn
is a kookaburra dawn –
awakened
with such optimism
I open wide the window

sunny and mild
this coastal winter
magnolias
already in bloom,
lawn-mowers droning

on the porch
I'm contemplating
my invitation
to the college luncheon
for 'Golden Graduates'

fifty years
since a ceremony
dispatched me
from Australian skies
to grey Nagoya

this wanderer
returns in old age
to her sea
of origin, basking
again beneath the blue

6. Outsinging Summer

in this dawn sky
even parrots look black –
the fire
in his mind has died
ashes to ashes

autumn breezes
through opened windows
tapping blinds…
the year advances,
no going back now

early March
in Hyde Park's thick leaves
cicadas
outsinging their summer,
rainbows in the fountain

one seagull
strutting a windy beach,
one swimmer
breasting white-tipped waves –
nothing stays the same

still day, yet
the sunset light is dimming
amid the cries
of birds in their night trees –
time to call it curtains

7. Bold Gold

this month
the mimosa bushes
colonising
our plain, cluttered, suburb
have come into their own

in bloom they sway
through blue September breezes
blowing perfume
from bright flower puffs
across the paths of our lives

their bold gold
flaunts itself round the frailty
of pale pink
plum blossoms on slender limbs
lifting higher in the sky

only magpies
carolling resplendent
on eucalypts
are as insistent that they
bring the spirit of spring

8. At Shell Harbour
south of Sydney, October 2014

dawn birds
sounds of the ocean
salted air –
my opened window
presents a coastal day

early morning
the beach belongs to dogs,
their devotees,
walkers, runners, and
wet-suited board riders

a blue-green surf
rolls in, breaks on white shore
rolls in, breaks
where children jump and squeal
on the spring strand at noon

dusk misting
as a southerly breeze stirs
the ebb tide
leaving sand damp and cool
shells sharp under bare feet

stars sparkle
into the sea's mystery
a moon-path
ripples from horizon
to deep-sleeping dunes

Tanka chains written with Mari Konno, published bilingually in
The Tanka Journal 2014–2015, edited by Aya Yuhki (Parts 1, 2
and 3 appeared in *Conversations in Tanka*, 2014, Amelia Fielden,
Jan Foster and Friends)

Summer Here, Winter There, Part 4

eve
of another year
what will
they be wishing for,
my friends near and far

                        A

far-dwelling
my friend has sent back
a tanka
in response to mine,
like an indigo echo

                        M

echo
of my thoughts, this
drumming rain;
what can I do now,
what should I do now

                        A

now they still
hold onto those tablets
I sent them
for radiation poisoning
three whole years earlier

                        M

Summer Here, Winter There, Part 5

earlier
than I had wished it
my daughter
became independent,
yet she asks my advice

          A

advice
could be dangerous
to tanka
I feel, while correcting
my students' works

          M

works of art
flown across the world
to our gallery
bringing new pleasures
new understanding

          A

understanding
one another deeply
we were waving
at the airport, only
separated by fences

          M

Summer Here, Winter There, Part 6

fences, hedges
walls…so many dividers
in this world,
while our feathered friends
have the freedom of the sky

                                      A

sky
and the moon
reflected
on each surface of rice paddies –
could Japan be a peaceful nation

                                      M

nation
after nation, menaced
by terrorism –
my husband overcome
now by senility

                                      A

senility
advancing in Mother –
midnight
I am her fatigued carer,
older than retirement age

                                    M

Tanka chain written with Mari Konno, published bilingually in
The Tanka Journal, 2016, edited by Aya Yuhki

Just Perfect

dawn garden
drenched with orange blossom
this prospect
of a poetry day
…just perfect

    A

perfect blue
the autumn sky
I remember
on a night train
in snowy December

    M

December
in North America
the days so dark
my heart so light
visiting family

    A

family reunion
on New Year's day
a 90 year-old
and a newborn baby
exchange smiles

    M

'smiles
of a Summer Night'
long ago
Ingmar Bergman movie
smiles from my student life

                            A

life
so vivid but absent
for long years –
dinosaur footprints
of a mother and a baby

                            M

baby panda
as cute as a stuffed toy
knows only
its mother in a cage
far from bamboo forests

                            A

forests gone
now forests of skyscrapers
are swaying
in this earthquake country
of Japanese islands

                            M

islands of hope
in the sea of despair
sometimes
there is light in his eyes
and a smile on his face
                          A

face down
I think of a forest
where
branches are pure white
with this winter's first snow
                          M

'snow day'
means school is cancelled
in the city
children play outdoors
regardless of the cold
                          A

cold light
appears in the east
to start
the new year's day
of this quake-prone country
                          M

New Zealand

a tanka tale published in *Downunder Japan*, vol. 2, 2015, edited by Graham Bathgate (Yūko's poems were translated by Amelia Fielden; 'poet and Empress' is an original tanka of Amelia's)

Two Spoonfuls

When poet Kawano Yūko, of humble birth but golden talent, lay dying in her Kyoto home, the Empress of Japan dispatched there from her Tokyo palace a courtier bearing a message of concern, and a container of restorative soup. Herbal soup Empress Michiko had prepared herself.

Too ill for appetite, yet conscious of the honour bestowed on her, Yūko tried to drink a little of the soup.

And before her eyes closed for the last time, she dictated these tanka poems to her daughter, Koh.

> *while the Empress's message*
> *that touched on tanka from my books*
> *'Reed Boat' and 'The Maternal Line',*
> *is read aloud to me, I try*
> *sipping at the soup she has sent*
>
> *bidden by her Majesty*
> *to take even two spoonfuls,*
> *at last, finally*
> *I have managed to finish*
> *sipping just those two spoonfuls*

A fable? A legend?

No, a small bowl of twenty-first century Japanese reality.

>   poet and Empress
>   both schooled and skilled in tanka
>   holding fast to threads
>   of this tradition woven
>   thirteen hundred years ago

individual tanka published in *Kokako*, late 2010–2012, edited by Patricia Prime and Joanna Preston; 2013–2015, edited by Patricia Prime and Margaret Beverland

       snow-white feathers
       on the wings of a dove
       ruffled
       by light blue breezes,
       we wait, this dove and I

~~~~

       seated beneath
       perfumed clouds of purple
       wisteria
       celebrating in spring
       the autumn of our lives

~~~~

       heart to heart
       we lie these cool nights
       so many years
       since we ran together
       along deep-leafed trails

~~~~

this bright morning
a rainbow lorikeet
on our lawn,
perfectly feathered
no breath in its body

~ ~ ~ ~

capricious spring
dark clouds and scudding winds
just when
the flowers and I
felt ready to bloom

~ ~ ~ ~

oh those shoes
bright turquoise killer heels,
oh those legs
long and slender and young –
my sandals stomp the staircase

~ ~ ~ ~

pale green carpet:
our hopes for a new start
in a new house
stained by spilt orange juice
and my angry reaction

~ ~ ~ ~

such sweetness
I'd never tasted
before
Hawaiian pineapple,
my second marriage

~ ~ ~ ~

when did he start
walking so slowly?
years and years
of fast strides, and now
what's the rush, he complains

~ ~ ~ ~

the clock ticking
a light plane circling,
between them
my too-quiet life
today and tomorrow

~ ~ ~ ~

Forgotten Lane
a signpost by the pines…
some paths
not taken, others mapped
in fading memory

~ ~ ~ ~

not expecting
a colony of black swans
at the jetty
I contemplate the nature
of this random world

~ ~ ~ ~

an old refrain
'love me or leave me'
if only
it were that simple…
star-bright nights continue

~ ~ ~ ~

sand in the bath
sunhat under the bed
the fading scent
of a shampoo she used,
all we have of her now

~ ~ ~ ~

the sad ending
of a novel we both loved
releasing my tears
at last I weep for you
and all we had shared

~ ~ ~ ~

a responsive tanka string written with Owen Bullock (New Zealand) published in *Kokako* 20, 2014, edited by Patricia Prime and Margaret Beverland (Owen's tanka are printed in italics)

The Lore of Lighthouses

divided outlines
beyond the slats
splay in the wind –
in bed for how long
my fever and I

Year of the Snake,
fifth time round since by birth,
did not bring
the good health I may need
to enjoy the sixth time

I know a man who said
'I'm not gonna let some star
push me around' –
he drove a bulldozer
during the day

raised
on the lore of lighthouses
and ancestors
who kept their lamps burning,
I have no fear of tempests

individual tanka published in *Kokako*, 2013–2015, edited by Patricia Prime and Margaret Beverland

>the glory
>of orange glass vases
>aligned
>luminous in summer sun
>my grandsons' smiles

>~ ~ ~

>will lilacs
>smell sweeter elsewhere?
>I linger
>hopefully, in your garden
>remembering old songs

>~ ~ ~

>once a week
>for thirty brief minutes
>our voices join
>while the ocean between us
>is rolled away

>~ ~ ~

waking early
surrounded by love
I regret
neither your urgent hands
nor our dogs' happy greetings

~~~~

Sunday jazz:
dancing fewer numbers
as time goes by
your rhythm slower
no longer matching mine

~~~~

on the white blind
a pattern of branches
shifting
from concern to concern
how can I clear my mind

~~~~

counting
the fingers and toes
on her new-born,
what mother doesn't do that –
twenty, the sum of relief

~ ~ ~ ~

just before dawn
in ragged chorus
kookaburras
shatter the silence –
turn to me now, my love

a tanka strand published in *Kokako*, 2015

Home Again

every night
I dream of you here
smiling
through the years of change…
then comes the dawn

hydrangea
varieties, so different
from each other –
must I now forsake
one of my lifestyles

home again
just to sell this place, I see
hibiscus
blooming their scarlet best
at the bedroom windows

on the front path
lies a parrot, no blood
on its plumage –
where do birds go
when they die

a great canvas
stretched between dark branches,
brilliant orange
splashed with blue and gold
the western sky at six

a responsive tanka string written with *Genie Nakano* (USA)
published in *Kokako*, 2015

Unusual Shells

melons
bursting on the vine
dripping
with sweetness, our eyes
cling to each other

summer evenings
lingering on the deck
in a soft haze
we sip chilled moscato,
defer the dream-time

over there
war still raging, you leave
tomorrow –
Lady of the Night in bloom
just until the sunrise

at low tide
I wander the warm sands
searching
for unusual shells
to show you, whenever…

individual tanka published in *Kokako*, 2016 and 2017, edited by Patricia Prime and Margaret Beverland

loosely wrapped
in crinkled silver foil
this lake today
concealing its secrets
as I conceal mine

~ ~ ~ ~

an old man sits
hunched over our table
ponderously
reading the newspaper –
where is my life-partner now

~ ~ ~ ~

'the ties that bind'
love at the end of the leash
strengthens
as his tug weakens
with the passing years

~ ~ ~ ~

a responsive tanka string written with *Giselle Maya* (France)
published in *Kokako*, 2016

Sarudoshi: The Year of the Monkey, 2016

the cheeky face
of my ten-year-old grandson
beaming
Happy New Year wishes
across the world on Facebook

his blue eyes sparkle
his smile is open and clear
his field notes cheer me
he draws birds from nature
this dear grandson of mine

a flotilla
of pink-billed pelicans
escorts
the fishing fleet's return
to their blue morning harbour

painting a garden bench
you lie on the cold earth
not feeling chilled
through a tear in your jeans
your knee peers at the sun

sun out again
after four days of rain
the sands are splashed
with rainbow colours
from beach umbrellas

snow country
in a hut built of snow
for prayers
a young monkey joins
children in padded haori

and another – this responsive string was written with *Jan Foster* (Australia) and published in *Kokako*, 2016

This Domestic Life

Christmas trees
slumped between garbage cans,
Christmas lights
stowed in the garage,
have last year's hopes been binned?

on my morning walk
it's hard to ignore
this sunrise
lighting the day ahead
with new possibilities

into her mouth
scrape off her chin
into her mouth
feeding mashed banana
to my daughter's daughter

the back patio
stained by purple splotches
hard to remove
those blackbirds
who love our blueberries

my shifting heart
chooses another lover
then another,
still staying loyal
to my golden Labrador

no regrets
at this final parting
as I drive away
in my new car
leaving behind my old one

a responsive tanka string written with *Jan Foster*, published in *Kokako*, 2018

Moorings

line of sight:
deep blue lake, white sail boat
spruce forest
mountain peaks, unclouded sky –
just this, for now

subtle warmth
of treasure spread out
on the pages
so much of value said
in so few words

one daughter
only phones or emails me,
the other
goes with pen, paper, and stamp –
years flow on, love is constant

at uni
I faced piles of paper,
today
my granddaughter
does it all on line

years and years
of busy family life
followed
by Facebook, and a dog
in silence at my feet

alone again
I slip my moorings
setting off
to find the way
back to myself

three tanka tales published in *Kokako*, 2017, edited by Patricia Prime and Margaret Beverland

Autumn Garden

lavender blue
dilly dilly, lavender green
you'll be
my King, dilly dilly
and I'll be your Queen*

Early in the season when Simon is moved to the secure dementia wing, his new room has a broad lavender bush blooming in the picture window.

Lavender and more lavender lines the paths rambling around the fenced garden where we linger while the sun still shines.

'What's that?' he points again and again.

I break off sprigs from the pale purple flowers, crush them between my fingers and offer their fragrance to his strongest remaining sense.

A few more wobbly paces, then Simon stumbles. He's weary; I need to get him back to his room.

Safely installed in his red velvet recliner chair, Simon slips into sleep.

once we reigned
together, over home and hearth
children and pets –
all mine now, this domain,
though the King still breathes

* This is one stanza of a version of the late seventeenth century traditional English nursery rhyme 'Lavender Blue'.

Going For It

At seventeen months unwanted, unloved, until he walked into my daughter's arms. Until he clambered onto my knee to share a chocolate mousse. Until we bounced him in the pool, singing 'The Wheels of the Bus'.

Years flow by.

> *pink peonies*
> *at the spring market*
> *helping him*
> *choose birthday flowers*
> *for his second mother*

Turned eleven, sporty and competitive, he passes one older boy after another in the final straight of a 3,000-metre race on track.

Afterwards, grinning with pride at a personal best, he says, 'I could hear you yelling 'go Stevo', so I went for it.'

> *some day*
> *I won't be here to cheer*
> *dearest boy*
> *remember my voice*
> *remember I loved you*

Full Circle

summer garden
magenta dahlias
rise regally
above the wild daisies
worlds away from childhood

My father taught me so much: the names of colours, of flowers, of dog breeds, of musical instruments, and many other things.

Speaking no language but English, his facility and fascination with precise terminology ultimately influenced my word-based career choice.

> *today, coaching*
> *my grandson in Scrabble*
> *I awe him*
> *with the obscurities*
> *Dad had at his command*

Serbia

an abbreviated tanka sequence published bilingually, in Serbian and English in *Haiku Novine*, issue 27, December 2012, edited by Dragan J. Ristic

'When I Grow Too Old To Dream'*

what shall I say
when we meet once more,
the lie
that I am happy
you're happy without me?

the warm light
on persimmon branches
over white walls –
falling in love again
I can't help it**

your silence
seems impenetrable
 this time
I won't be seduced
into speaking first

translucent waves
rolling towards the shore
gradually
I have come to see
we'll never be lovers

* 'I will have this to remember' quoted from the popular song with music by Sigmund Romberg and lyrics by Oscar Hammerstein, published in 1934
** 'Falling in Love Again' (Can't Help It) is the English language name for a 1930 German song by Friedrich Holloender originally performed by Marlene Dietrich, who also recorded it in English.

individual tanka published (with Serbian translations) in the Serbian haiku magazine *Osvit*, 2015, edited by Milenko D. Cirovic Ljuticki

long avenue
a great sweep of concrete
beneath bare trees –
spring will come again
but not for my three friends

~ ~ ~ ~

one seagull
strutting the autumn beach,
one swimmer
breasting the white-tipped waves…
nothing stays the same

~ ~ ~ ~

again today
you could not remember
my name –
it is already dark
and there are few stars

~ ~ ~ ~

USA

two tanka published in *All the Shells*, Anthology of the Tanka Society of America, 2014, edited by M. Kei

>widening ripples
>as we breaststroke slowly
>across the lake
>the child confides she might
>search for her birth mother

~~~~

>in despair
>after her letter
>I sit up late
>watching detectives
>solve their case on screen

~~~~

and one published in *Spent Blossoms*, Anthology of the Tanka Society of America, 2015, edited by Claire Everett

>wheatsheaf hair
>hiding her face, she sleeps,
>this granddaughter
>I never thought I'd have
>such a stake in the future

individual tanka published in *Atlas Poetica: A Journal of Place*, 2011–2015, edited by M. Kei and known from 2015 as *Atlas Poetica: A Journal of World Tanka*

at the marina, dashing, flashing
Ballard, like turquoise needles
Seattle, dragonflies
USA transparent wings whirring
over dark still waters

~ ~ ~ ~

Seattle bluer than blue
in the sparkling afternoon
Lake Washington
like endless lengths of brocade
unrolled from the floating bridge

~ ~ ~ ~

spring pond
black swan paddling
with five cygnets
against a backdrop
of crab apple blossom

~ ~ ~ ~

        smooth highway
        driving between pine forests
        in Oregon
        distant from contemplation
        of your particular concerns

~~~~

Cannon Beach,   bright blue day
Oregon, USA   the child flying her kite
                   at high tide
                   sea filling sandcastle moats
                   …a squabble of seagulls

~~~~

White Fish,   immensely long
Montana,   a freight train rounds the bend –
USA   surely that
                   will have the capacity
                   to transport my woes away

~~~~

University House,   light dazzles
Canberra,   reflected from the pool
Australia   onto the ceiling
of a long veranda –
orange koi swim, heads down

~ ~ ~ ~

Canberra   golden wattle
above frost's silver
another August
I will leave you knowing
I'm bound to come back

~ ~ ~ ~

Sydney,   'roll up, roll up
Australia   for all the fun of the fair
try your luck…'
and when this carousel slows,
will my luck run out?

~ ~ ~ ~

Sydney   'in France
I never dream, for France
is the dream,'
she tells me, gazing beyond
our sapphire ocean

~ ~ ~ ~

Buff Point, the house agent
Australia asks how far we want to live
from garbage dumps
and power stations – not
how close to beach or forest

~ ~ ~ ~

night frost
on crystal windows
before sunrise
sky tinged lime green –
how to embrace this day

~ ~ ~ ~

earth hour:
electricity switched off
we look younger
by candlelight recalling
the way we were

~ ~ ~ ~

Terrigal,   gospel service:
Australia   behind the trumpeter
                     a candle flame
                     sways to Swing Low
                     and then The Old Rugged Cross

~ ~ ~ ~

Tokyo,   city hotel
Japan   the scenery a weeping willow
                     hard against
                     a stained concrete wall
                     guarding overhead train tracks

~ ~ ~ ~

from Canberra   we speak
to Tokyo   long distance of daily matters
                     all the while
                     I sense we are as close
                     as we were years ago

tanka published in *Atlas Poetica* special feature issues, 2012–2017

Snipe Rising from a Marsh: *Birds in Tanka*, 2012, edited by Rodney Williams

> in the reeds
> a red-winged blackbird sings
> for its mate…
> so little response
> from you, to my emails

Ekphrastic Tanka, 2012, edited by Patricia Prime

> sculpted in bronze
> seven giant pears, unchanged
> unlike
> the vanished children
> I photographed there

The Garage, Not the Garden: Tanka of Urban Life, 2013, edited by M. Kei

> at Joe's café
> the coffee afternoon
> grinds on, while
> flies laze around the dregs
> of our poetry

Geography and the Creative Imagination, 2014, edited by Sonam Chhoki

> a crocodile
> of schoolgirls, winding
> down Gallery Road
> accompanying me
> scores of memories

Arthropods, 2017, edited by Grunge

> establishing
> its web behind the sensor
> a house spider
> sets off the alarm –
> all power to nature

An experimental collaborative tanka tale, renku-style, using four key words, in a form developed by Marilyn Humbert, leader of the Australian Bottlebrush Tanka Group. This piece was written by Neal Whitman (nw) and Amelia Fielden (af) and published in *Atlas Poetica: A Journal of World Tanka*, 2016, edited by M. Kei.

Weather…or Not

Who trusted God was love indeed
And loved Creation's final law
Tho' **Nature**, **red** in **tooth** and **claw**
With ravine, shriek'd against his creed
Alfred, Lord Tennyson,
'In Memoriam, A.H.H.', canto 56

1.

still salty
from morning sea swim
I call
the grandkids at the end
of their snow skiing day   af

2. Warm Wishes

An Italian poet emails me New Year wishes. She includes her photograph of mimosa blooming at the end of December in the gardens of San Remo where it is unseasonably warm. I forward the mimosa to a friend in Australia and learn in reply that there it is known as wattle.

bird-like Lydia
in hand-dyed purple clothing
flitting here and there
she spreads pollen and seeds
with scrolling arabesques   nw

3. Nothing Stays the Same

A cyclone uproots our honey-gem grevillea, which topples onto the veranda. When nature shines again tree-loppers arrive in brightly coloured safety vests to break its branches and remove the tree corpse.

> a wild clan
> of rainbow lorikeets
> searching
> in neighbourhood gardens
> new sources of sustenance   af

4. What's in a Name

We treat ourselves to the La Bibloteca room wrapped in terracotta shades of Venetian Plaster. Here at the Smith-Madrone vineyards high up on Spring Mountain in St Helena, the vines are planted on very steep slopes in red Aiken soil which is derived from weathered volcanic materials and sedimentary rock. Breakfast conversation centres on the drought, now in its fifth year. Our host remarks, 'It's been a normally bizarre year.'

> the store clerk murmurs
> nuanced with olive flavour
> I am befuddled
> so I focus on the names
> and choose The Curator   nw

5. The Temerity of Wildflowers

First experiences of the 'Mediterranean diet' in its natural setting come with a two year posting to Malta.

There I fall in love with wild freesias in spring, the intensity of the island's dry six-month-long summers, the violence of winter storms, my friend's husband.

> this tideless sea
> is a placid turquoise,
> this tideless sea
> is a turbulent grey –
> my secret thoughts stay secret

6. Sunshine on My Shoulder

In 1962 there was an animated TV show about a futuristic family, The Jetsons, where dad George Jetson commuted to work in an 'aerocar' that resembled a flying saucer with a bubble top. As a fourteen-year-old, I wondered how they avoided mid-air collisions.

This morning on the TV Ag Report I learn that agricultural drones are causing problems for commercial flights in and out of our local Monterey Airport.

> John Denver
> crashed his Long-EZ aircraft
> into Monterey Bay*
> on that date we gather there
> and sing Whose Garden Was This?   nw

---

* 13 October 1997

7. Missing

Our dear old dog, Kin, is missing a tooth.

Whether he lost it crashing into the iron-barred gate…now he has only blurred vision…or whether he'd tried to chomp on a long-buried bone, we don't know. But his lopsided grin is rather cute, and he can manage to wolf down his meals as usual.

> fifteen years
> I have felt his heart beating
> in my lap
> I'll hold him when the time comes
> for the beat to slow and stop   af

8. Males Generally Are Larger

I am a guest professor at the John Hopkins School of Medicine. The medical residents take me to lunch at the Crab Shack, and do the ordering. There on a white paper plate on the table a Maryland blue crab stares at me and I stare back. There is no silverware on the table. What to do? I look up at a round of smirks. One of the young whippersnappers shows me how to remove the 'dead man's fingers' (the gills), snap the body down the centre, and pull off the claws. Then, from a glass jar in the middle of the table, one of my hosts hands me a wooden mallet to crack open the critter and eat with my fingers.

> I learn the shell
> of female crabs is edged
> bright orange
> and both sexes walk sideways –
> good tips for finding a mate   nw

9. The Threads that Bind

Perhaps we might have mated for life. And in that era lots of our friends were marrying young, soon after university graduation. But before he can propose I am offered my ambitious heart's desire, a scholarship for research in Kyoto. For my birthday he gives me a book about Japan. 'With love from…' is inscribed on a blank page. 'That's so you can tear it out if you want to forget me,' he explains.

> how could I
> ever forget my best friend?
> home and abroad
> last century and this
> we stay connected still   af

> 10.
> tides rising, falling,
> many man-made boundaries
> now erased –
> we are stewards of this Earth
> and its climate is changing   nw

a collaborative tanka string written with Genie Nakano,
published in *Atlas Poetica*, issue 25, 2016, edited by M. Kei

Pouring Out Tears

phone conversation
on a spring afternoon
we listen
to my backyard wind-chimes,
a stranger and I

                G

*he does not know
who I am, only that
the music
played by the orchestra
is pleasing us both*

                A

let's go
alchemistic, turn
dark corners
dig through trash cans
searching for gold

                G

*silver threads
in his golden plume
of a tail —
the least of my concerns
when I'm playing the vet's bill*

                A

his brown eyes
see right through me
as he sniffs
out all of my love,
this little rescue dog

         G

'rescue yourself'
urge friends and family
while forty years
of loving partnership
smash on dementia's shores

         A

if I lose my memory
walk me through
our home,
pick up all the laughter,
pour out all the tears

         A

a collaborative tanka string written with *Kathabela Wilson*,
published in *Atlas Poetica*, issue 26, 2016, edited by M. Kei

Safe Harbour

lulled to sleep
in a pine tree's giant arms,
I awake
with the sun glinting silver
over the morning harbour

                                        A

forty years since
I ferried past
Lady Liberty
I began my own life
cross-continent

                                        K

Australia
smallest continent
largest island
in the world where I am
to live without you

                                        A

a figure of humour
and strange beauty
I posed myself
driftwood and stone
on the California shore

                             K

coarse grey sand
strewn with driftwood logs
the Seattle shore,
far from Coogee's white beach,
becomes my second home

                             A

shall I choose
to go back to the beginning
or is it better
to keep memory full
of what might have been

                             K

a collaborative tanka string written with *Jan Foster* published in
Atlas Poetica, issue 28, 2017, edited by M. Kei

All That Energy

moonshone
the playground slide glitters
beside stilled swings –
all that energy
'here today, gone tomorrow'

taking the lift
instead of the stairs
this race
through life costing me
more than I have to spare

as days draw in
gold wattle blooms through winter
softening
the rocky escarpment –
is this our best time, perhaps

a visit with my mum
at the aged care home –
she thanks me,
asks who I am
…for the third time

one more shift hour
at the hospice for Mark
then home
to his bed-bound partner
and a bottle of red

a flight of pelicans
wings its way
across the horizon
stitching a neat seam
through tangerine sunset

a tanka tale published in *Atlas Poetica*, issue 28, 2017, edited by M. Kei

From the East

Windy this early afternoon, Wollongong is luminous in primary colours: green escarpment, green park, blue lagoon, blue ocean, blue sky…

I drift back to the orange sunrises I watched through the window beside my bed in a hotel where we stayed last December.

>*flame-coloured*
>*hot over the horizon*
>*those dawns*
>*of my seventy-fifth year*
>*on the coast where I was born*

That holiday season just six months ago still cradled a vestige of hope for our future together

>*from the east*
>*comes a strong summer sun:*
>*Christmas Day*
>*in the Tasman Sea*
>*'all is calm, all is bright'*

But the new year has brought us not a fresh start, only an ending. Yet relaxing into this painterly day, I can see that all is not black and white…or even grey.

>*no more longing,*
>*I will absorb this loss*
>*in my life*
>*I have loved so many —*
>*the sun sets, the sun rises*

two tanka sequences published in *Atlas Poetica*, 2017/2018, edited by M. Kei

Sunday At Lake Ginninderra

so little movement
in the silent sparkling lake
this cool morning
no ball-mad ginger poodle
is plunging through the ripples

no wild splashing
no wavelets in her wake –
a swan appears
leading cygnets in peace
from shore to empty shore

there's a body
by the reeds a flat grey fish –
instinctively
I mouth the command 'leave it'
to a dog who isn't there

the heft and fire
of that aquatic creature
are light ashes now
settled in a ginger jar
at the lakeside home we shared

No Moon At All

lying here
alone but not lonely
in a soft bed
the sleeping hours drift by,
what will the wind do now

pale snow light
through half-opened blinds
silhouettes
his concentration…
morning piano practice

one black bird
perched in a tall bare tree –
can't start
weeping and wailing
in case I never stop

Beethoven's Ninth
from the student choirs
pure voices
assailing the heavens
on Christmas Eve

far away
across the sea, the fragrance
of eucalypt
recalls where I come from
where I must return

somewhere
through the dark still night
this wistful tune
from a harmonica:
'no moon at all'

a collaborative tanka tale, published in *Atlas Poetica*, 2018, edited by M. Kei

Weather Uncertain, Conditions Unknown

Neal Whitman (prose) and Amelia Fielden (tanka)

Lighthouses are endlessly suggestive signifiers of both human isolation and our ultimate connectedness to each other

Virginia Woolf

> *to save ships*
> *and all who sail in them*
> *lighthouses*
> *at the world's flashpoints…*
> *what is there warning us now*

I was reading a group of poems by Eugenio Montale, Finisterre. Aha! I fathom these have something to do with the end of land… land's end! I search the internet and learn that, on the Galicia coast in northwest Spain, Faro de Cabo Finisterre is the most westerly lighthouse on the European continent.

My wife and I once stayed in the lighthouse keeper's cottage at the Point Arena Lighthouse on California's Mendocino coast and were told it sits on a spit of land that is the closest point of the Lower 48 to Hawaii…thus, our most westerly lighthouse.

Next, I wondered about the most easterly lighthouse in the U.S. and learned that it is the West Quoddy Head Light in Lubec, Maine. It turns out that the greatest distance between any two mainland points within the contiguous 48 states is 2,892 miles: Point Arena to West Quoddy Head! And it is another 2,814 miles from West Quoddy Head Light to Faro de Cabo Finisterre.

We ponder: what if those three lighthouses could send out a warning to Planet Earth:

DANGER, PROCEED WITH CAUTION

What if those three lighthouses could coordinate a Morse Code signal?

Point Arena Lighthouse…   at 6pm Pacific Standard Time

West Quoddy Light Head ---   at 9.01pm Eastern Standard Time

Faro de Cabo Finisterre…   at 3.02am Central European Time

Imagine a continuous loop of repetitive lighthouse flashes until day breaks on the West coast of Spain.

SOS repeated over and over.

Imagine the message live-streamed on the internet that Earth is in danger. Proceed with caution.

> *into the dark*
> *sweep after sweep of light beams*
> *illuminates*
> *the perils of our shores,*
> *of our complacency*

individual tanka published in *Bright Stars: An Organic Tanka Anthology*, volumes 1–6, focusing on the Japanese aesthetic of Akarui – bright, light, 2014, edited by M. Kei

let's quickly drink
this New Year's pink champagne
for
we might not die tomorrow
but then again we might

~~~~

he would say this
is a perfect afternoon
for sailing,
and I'd shake my head –
the power of veto

~~~~

luncheon break:
several poets confess
they're composing,
switched off from the speakers
at this staid conference

~~~~

Meryl Streep
Judi Dench, fine actors
even finer
as they age – wish I could
say the same for myself

~~~~

lolling
on her woolly back
a white poodle
seduces the master
of her new family

~ ~ ~ ~

your desires
are my desires
no longer –
so what now will we call
our 'many-splendoured thing'?

~ ~ ~ ~

north-west summer
light lingering till late
on their deck
the sweetness of children
and cherry ice cream

~ ~ ~ ~

mid July
the lavender suburbs
on vacation –
plucking flower heads
the child says 'smell my hands'

~ ~ ~ ~

one of us
has a swollen left foot
two have bad knees
the fourth never could dance,
yet we do, when the jazz band plays

~ ~ ~ ~

we talk now
of health issues, friends
your grandchildren…
'you told me you loved me
when we were young that day'

~ ~ ~ ~

which to choose
raspberry ripple or
peppermint…
a senior's dilemma
at the ice cream counter

~ ~ ~ ~

seventy-two…
how has this happened to me
constantly
rehearsing my life,
not ready to act old

~ ~ ~ ~

sparkles
sail down the stream –
this is how
she writes her poetry,
her poetry, not mine

~~~~

a week's rain
and the paddocks are green,
complacent,
I feel certain too
our drought has broken

~~~~

thank you
Alexander Bell, today
distant grandkids
called to read for us
some stories they'd written

~~~~

autumn willows
golden threads cascading
to a river
dappled with cloud shadow
rippled with singing

~~~~

'where do I sign?'
asked just as eagerly
at the church
and fourteen years later
in the divorce court

~ ~ ~ ~

the clear flow
of birdsong trickles away
as the stream
disappears down the drain –
how long since he last wrote

~ ~ ~ ~

glass half empty
he starts another day –
how long can I
carry my full one
without spilling our lives

~ ~ ~ ~

fossicking
in the grassy puddle
a blue heron –
my Gran, always grateful
for life's little things

~ ~ ~ ~

a responsive tanka string written with *Kath Abela Wilson* and published in *Bright Stars: An Organic Tanka Journal*, 2014, edited by M. Kei

Fire Basket

does the cormorant
feel a sadness
I give back
what I thought I had
again and again

their wedding photo
with all the loving family
we had back then,
makes me too aware
of the absences now

under morning's red bridge
our sweetfish
at the festival
shadows touch
as a lantern swings

no shadow
in our living room
we sit
apart together watching
the bright lights on TV

our translucent hearts
painted on the inside
bone china
we watch as the light goes on
in the waiting room

tea and talk
the universal language
of sharing –
I count the weeks till
arrival at Narita

pressed flowers
in my overflowing book
always open
I add more fallen petals
as I continue our conversation

regretting
I didn't keep a journal
in Japan
fifty years ago
my wedding bouquet, all pink

expectant sizzle
of okonomiyaki
our third marriage
of dance of bonito flakes
and green onion

individual tanka published in *cattails: collected works of the United Haiku and Tanka Society*, 2015, edited by an'ya

fastening
my aquamarine earrings
I gaze out
at the vast azure sky…
my most loved tones, these blues

~ ~ ~ ~

how close
the herringbone fern grows
to a tree trunk –
I never expected
her marriage would flourish

~ ~ ~ ~

behind your voice
the constant shirring
of cicadas
and our twenty years
of communication

~ ~ ~ ~

parents long passed
progeny independent
I entered
my seventh decade
vibrating with doubt

~ ~ ~ ~

through thick mist
over the lake a kayak
glides silently
into the willow-lined shore
into the looming winter

~ ~ ~ ~

a tanka published in *Caught in the Breeze*, Fifth Haiku Pacific Rim Conference Anthology, 2012, edited by Susan Antolin

> a tiny cloud
> in the summer-blue sky –
> should I use
> pen or pencil for events
> in next year's diary

and one published in the Haiku North America Anthology, 2013

> the hill street here
> is lined with cherry trees
> yaezakura
> deep pink double blossoms –
> Japan feels far away

individual tanka published in *Fire Pearls: Short Masterpieces of Love and Passion*, vol. 2, 2013, edited by M. Kei

seldom touching
deeply, impossibly
in love, we were
like the protagonists
of a Victorian novel

~~~~

two pelicans
side by side at low tide
barely paddling,
floating on the here and now
our backs to the horizon

~~~~

oxygen masked
were you going to die
right there
beside me on the plane
where I couldn't kiss you

~~~~

while you lived
I disguised my passion,
now I mourn
as appropriate
for a family friend

~~~~

moon obscured
by high-rise buildings
the street lamps
light my way home
to 'true romance'

~ ~ ~ ~

at three a.m.
throwing off the blanket
I turn away…
this is not the kind of heat
our relationship needs

~ ~ ~ ~

a cage
with its door propped open
is still a cage…
fun afternoon over, I scurry
home to cook your dinner

~ ~ ~ ~

Monday's wash
flapping on the clothes' line
stainless…
now to scrub out
my memories of marriage

~ ~ ~ ~

three tanka tales published in *Haibun Today*, electronic journal, 2017, edited by Janet L. Davis

Frost At the Vineyard

It seems I have had to travel a very long way to make peace with my situation at home. Back there the summer heat has already begun. Here in northern California russet and gold autumn lingers in the trees while a light frost spikes underfoot. The sky is a wide, blue, wash. A myriad of tiny white-crowned sparrows is darting to and fro, foraging in piles of black loam.

> *across the world*
> *my love is lost in himself –*
> *I lift my face*
> *to the winter sun*
> *this season of acceptance*

A piebald pony grazes on the still-wet grass. White goats lie folded in the fields.

The road the tour takes follows bold river curves, then slides under the shade of giant redwoods.

> *the great forest*
> *is never silent,*
> *simply quiet*
> *like a contemplative mind*
> *gently sifting its issues*

An hour later we see Russian River, broad and blue, joining the tumult of the Pacific Ocean.

Rising through salt spray, hawks wheel sidewards in the ferocious wind. I retreat to the other side of the dunes, sit on a driftwood log and write in my journal.

> *brown pelicans*
> *of California*
> *white pelicans*
> *of my distant country –*
> *at night I dream of wings*

The Rhythm of Life

White Fish Lake, Montana; July 2011. Six years ago. Such a short time, really.

Look at the man in the photo, a proud old salt, about to show his small grandson the way to paddle over the sunlit lake.

Look at the boy, smiling, entrusting himself to the strong arms of his grandpa.

Today the man is propped up in a nursing home bed, his dulled eyes wandering across the scenes in the video we are trying to show him. It's the grandson he does not recognise now racing his own kayak.

>   *the year turns*
>   *into another spring –*
>   *our star jasmine*
>   *no longer thrusts upwards*
>   *yet its perfume remains*

Another Morning

whitewashed house
behind high whitewashed walls
patterned purple
with bougainvillea –
the muezzin's call to prayer

Lying half asleep, I listen to the front door open and close. Then the garden gate.

In fifteen minutes or so, Fatima will be back from the French bakery at the end of the boulevard. She'll be laying the table for breakfast: a still warm baguette, butter from the slab in the market grocery, homemade apricot jam, juice squeezed from our own oranges, a pot of strong coffee…mmm.

I open my eyes and roll out of bed.

Alas – what I'd heard were not the sounds of morning at 14 Rue du Béarn, Agdal, but my husband and dogs setting out for a walk from our home in suburban Canberra, many years and many thousands of kilometres distant from Morocco.

the faint scent
of eucalyptus leaves…
wide awake
with longing – must have been
dreaming again in Arabic

individual tanka published in *Moonbathing: a journal of women's tanka*, 2011–2013, edited by Pamela A. Babusci

at our age
lingering on the line
just to listen
to each other's voices...
black night fills the windows

~~~~

my layered life...
today can I break through
emerge again
into the green garden
of creativity

~~~~

my breasts shrink
from the icy machine –
think survival
I tell myself, facing this
yearly examination

~~~~

my diary
is my life as I wish
to live it
free from unscheduled
tempers and demands

~~~~

so many hours
in a lonely day –
frangipani
scent intensifying
as the heat thickens

~~~~

tinsel grasses
along the highway
at journey's end
a swath of blue-ribbon sea
and you, waiting…

~~~~

the night is black
the wind blows violently
now a storm
of love arises
to vanquish our sleep

~~~~

a tanka string published in *Poems of the World: International Quarterly Magazine*, 2017, edited by Elma D. Photikarm

Spring At Last

the rain has stopped
I must go out to sweep
my courtyard –
trees weary of winter leaves
shedding them, begin to bud

star jasmine
tiny white flowers perfume
my garden,
purple wisteria drapes
the neighbour's fence…spring

in the greening park
grey-haired senior citizens,
arms and legs
moving slowly, slowly
through t'ai chi rhythm

cold days gone,
five scarlet flowers unfold
and baby birds
chirp insistently
from a hibiscus bush

twilight time
a single black swan
motionless
on the silver lake
softly framed by willow fronds

individual tanka published in *Portholes: Anthology of Tanka Sunday*, 2013, on the theme of 'water', edited by Michael Welch and Amelia Fielden

        blue dragonflies
        skimming a sun-dappled lake,
        silver seaplanes
        ascending a cloudless sky:
        the lightness of summer

~~~~

        with flowing manes
        white horses gallop rough seas
        beyond the calm
        of our tête-à-tête
        a tempest is roiling

~~~~

a responsive tanka string written by *Amelia* with Genie Nakano and published in *Ranpu Shimpo*, Los Angeles Japanese daily newspaper

Like Bamboo

the moon smiles
cracks up a dark sky
laughter
falls to the earth…
joy to the world

New Year dawns
at different times
through the world
most folk wishing for peace,
some intent on turmoil

this candle
burns for peace, my friend
keep it steady
focusing body and mind –
tonight the winds are strong

winds of chance
blow us this way and that
like bamboo
bending not breaking
we are held by the earth

the new year
a time for fresh beginnings…
my teacher, sensei
gently repeats 'flowers
always turn to the sun'

individual tanka published in *red lights*, 2011–2014, edited by Marilyn Hazelton

    a pelican
    and its reflection
    glide the lake
    past a cormorant's dive
    fish circles on the surface

~~~~

    I watch her face
    molded by forty-six years
    mourning her boy…
    'the anaesthetist
    made a mistake,' she says

~~~~

    along the limbs
    of an old peppercorn tree
    flit blue tits…
    there is no tomorrow,
    each day is today

~~~~

screeching seagulls
swoop for scraps on the pier
such a comfort
to swap sad stories
with her hand in mine

~ ~ ~ ~

at times
a sticky spiderweb
at times
a soft silken net,
this family enfolding me

~ ~ ~ ~

on a day
of disappointments
I'm delighted
by the discovery
amethysts can be green

~ ~ ~ ~

frame by frame
the weekend slides by
predictable
as his 'what's on today?'
and forgetting my answer

~~~~

a white heron
stands on its reflection
in the mirror lake
the stillness so needed
for my shifting heart

~~~~

the train's windows
weeping while I'm trying
to stay dry-eyed…
too many memories
along this line

~~~~

above the lake
standing still as statues
on a small pier
a large huddle of pelicans –
we all wait for something

~ ~ ~ ~

how I hate
clocks with a dominant tick
stridently
hacking away the hours –
I need more time, not less

~ ~ ~ ~

beneath willows
and weeping cherry trees
red tulips blaze
upright and smiling still
one more spring alive

~ ~ ~ ~

two tanka strings published in *red lights*, 2015

Walking the Dogs

wisteria
draped over a well-worn fence
purple,
favourite colour for clothes
in my seventies now

overlaid
with crinkled silver foil
this lake today
conceals its secrets
as I conceal mine

the sports field
is embroidered with tiny flowers,
those yellow daisies
we threaded into chains there
on long ago school days

belting out
their morning ballads
from the safety
of a tall eucalypt,
two shining magpies

the fragrance
of wild freesias
stirring
in neglected gardens…
I pause   the dogs run on

A Matter of Time

eucalypts
filled with birds, in dawn light
I see
how to handle today
today, not tomorrow

how long
this imprisonment
of marriage –
is there no parole
for good behaviour

'now only
a matter of time'
opines the doctor
wasn't it always
a matter of time

quiet rain
on the garden all night –
will the morning
be any different from
other dementia mornings

moonlight
slices through wooden blinds
night after night
I lie beside you
in silent despair

a responsive tanka string written with *Jan Foster*, published in *red lights*, 2016

Images

flashes of green
wild budgerigars
fluttering
from branch to branch to branch
the thoughts of a long night

skimming along
the tops of tall buildings
summer clouds
free of earthly moorings
…I wish I could fly

without wings
I am sardine-canned
across the world
to winter, warm hugs,
shining white birch trees

managing
the awkward moment
on a glissade
of icy politeness
I survive…

four together
in a ski gondola
up the slopes –
all those years wondering
whether she'd have children

two solo strings published in *red lights*, also in 2016

Just In Case

I continue
to coffee-spoon my life
circumspectly
keeping closed for now
that pandora's box

three roses
from a single stem – I
could compare them
to my children, though
one never bloomed

I will keep
all of their collars
just in case
there is a heaven
where we can live together

four years after
his diagnosis
of dementia
come birthday cards inscribed
Many Happy Returns

our old campus
with frog sounds from the creek
and high above
stars blazing like those nights
we couldn't stop kissing

Familiar Faces

gazing
through Monet window panes
of greening trees
on a blue and white sky,
I escape from my winter

when you and I
played house in the cubby
how innocent
we were of surgeries,
care homes, and all the rest

viewing
the green pottery pieces
as chopstick rests,
I live again for a while
in the place I was happiest

plum wine nights
scarlet maple days
in Japan
once more looking for love
among familiar faces

two tanka sequences published in *red lights*, 2017

Goodbye Again

scouring the shine
from a pewter lake
winter winds
scrape away the last leaves –
no one to hold my gloved hand

in his Care Home
weeks of babbling nonsense, then
he looks at me
and says 'I do love you' –
that's when I finally weep

nurse Adam
wears a diamond ear stud
and a bright smile
while he tends to those without
anything to hope for

gardenias
flowered by my front door,
their perfume
powerful for a time
before they decayed and dropped

his last gift
best he ever bought me
a painting
resembling our poodle –
soon I'll lose both man and dog

Not Yet

spring seems late
blossom trees are still in bud
just daffodils
and fast-growing grandkids
open their bright faces to me

daffodils
battered by the spring winds
this morning
we are each ragged –
piano practice again

the long years
I've been waiting, show
in the moss
on the garden gate,
in the white of the dog's face

pale landscape
cherry blossoms, grey sky
silver lake –
defying old age, I'll wear
purple, and a red hat

January 2014 *red lights* tanka inspiration

Readers were invited to meditate with this tanka by Mokichi Saito and reflect on the colour red

> *cosmos flowers*
> *swaying*
> *in twilight*
> *and that girl*
> *watching traces of light in the sky*
>
> Mokichi Saito

my tanka response

> when the poet* died
> the family forgot to plant
> her cosmos seeds…
> autumn came, sadder still
> without her favourite scarlet flowers

* The reference is to Kawano Yūko, 1946–2010.

individual tanka published in *Ribbons: Tanka Society of America Journal*, late 2010 to 2016, edited by David Rice

ten short years
since I sat by a lake
waiting –
you came too late
and with the wrong answer

~ ~ ~ ~

on the ring finger
of that handsome young man
offering his seat,
a gold wedding band –
I still notice such things

~ ~ ~ ~

a spring afternoon
at senior housing
silver voices
around the piano
singing of other homes

~ ~ ~ ~

a sudden gust
blows little brown birds
and russet leaves
from the autumn maple
into the cool blue sky

~ ~ ~ ~

my little dog
the velvety feel
of his skin
and his heart beating
on my bare thigh

~ ~ ~ ~

dawn blazing
behind giant eucalypts
yet a soft rain –
confused still by you
confused still by us

~ ~ ~ ~

comforted
I can still count in French
to one hundred,
I close the dementia book –
my cut roses look quite fresh

~ ~ ~ ~

there we were
burgundy curtains drawn,
sipping port
in the flickering firelight,
silenced by desire

~~~~

'no ice, please'
orders my daughter,
her passions
still undiluted
by illness or age

~~~~

wisteria
in mauve bunches dangling
beyond my reach
you fall into the twilight
of forgetfulness

~~~~

'no seasickness
if you watch the horizon' –
diagnosed
with dementia her husband
sees nothing good ahead

~~~~

beside me
on the long flight back
an empty seat –
telling myself I am
comfortable, not lonely

~~~~

beneath the aircraft
an expanse of wrinkled sea –
once home
how should I iron out
our relationship

~~~~

turned seventy
I see myself possibly
organising
my stamp collection
when I am older

~~~~

entangled
in a trawler net
of old age
with other by-catch
floundering despondently

~~~~

eight tanka strands published in *Ribbons*, 2014–2017, edited by David Rice

1. Unexpected

finding myself
still alive at dawn
finally
I drift off to sleep…
the doctor's voice fades

parallel
contrails on the pale blue sky –
sudden illness
forces the cancellation
of my trip to Osaka

overheard
from my hospital bed
'I'd rather
nurse children than adults,
kids are so much nicer'

2. December Downunder

heat shimmers
in the city centre
the Salvos' band
proclaiming 'Silent Night'
long before the first star

Seasons Greetings:
today's card carries
the message
from his wife that
my old lover is dying

grandchildren
hang baubles and tinsel
unevenly
the pine tree branch wilts
in spite of air conditioning

festive meal
of seafoods, salads, and
hot plum pudding –
a toast 'to absent friends'
in sparkling shiraz

rooftop tiles
ripple with sunshine
and shadows
from dusty eucalypts:
Christmas in summer

3. Buff Point Days

sometimes
kookaburras start
their laughing song
before the blush of dawn
colours the eastern sky

each morning
early, rainbow lorikeets
are here
feasting on the flowers
of our golden grevillea

later
as we walk by the lake
a blue heron
poses in the shallows
cormorants plunge for fish

perching
on the bridge's light poles
an absurdity
of pink-billed pelicans
waiting for the next delivery

scattered
among wild freesias
white cockatoos
foraging for seeds
in the clifftop grasses

fluffy clouds
of rose-breasted galahs
drift at dusk
over darkening trees
coming home to roost

there's a saying
'home is where the heart is'
yet my loves
are far and wide, flighty
as the birds of the air

4. Sun Shafts

my first lover
has Alzheimer's now
his wife says
he calls her by my name
on the beach of our past

lush bushes
of yellow roses
at her window
the widow insists
she's not really lonely

on his good days
rainbow lorikeets wake me
from our garden
the sky brightens to clear blue
on his good days

the 'new norm'
they call this limbo
every day
I take the dogs to visit
our man in L17

sun shafts
light up loved paintings
many mornings
of happiness here –
still the death toll rises

5. Incoming Tide

the past appears
a landscape of choices
I ventured
hopefully, here and there,
never quite arriving

I swim along
always on the surface
not daring
to explore what lies beneath
these dark ripples, this life

my present
of problems and dilemmas
made easier
only by daydreaming
of the unknowable

incoming tide
shallow pools of sea water
spread on the sand –
will I plunge through the surf
or retreat to the dunes

a cypress leans
away from the mist-grey wind
away from the ocean
I long to embrace
the waves and you, again

at the end
of our long straight road
an expanse
of blue shimmering –
'let's go, dear old dog'

6. But that was in another country, and besides…'*

purple-grey
twilight shopping street,
purple-grey gloves
made in Japan
this history…

canal path
in the gusty dusk
willows tremble –
I'm trying to forget
the sense of your letter

we sip wine
where once we loved
then step out
into the violet light
going our separate ways

drifting down
on my lilac umbrella
misty rain
and the plaintive twang
of a shamisen

by the roadside
silvering dandelions
on weak stems –
how could I give you
what you said you wanted

* from the play *The Jew of Malta*, by Christopher Marlowe, 1589

7. What I Once Had

still warm, yet
it's autumn already –
no kids there,
only cormorants
diving in the lake

summoned…
changing directions
changing speeds,
focused on getting there,
getting there in time

nothing more now
except the watching
the waiting
day and night,
night and day

as handsome
and cold as a stone King
in the Abbey
my working-class husband
beyond his last breath

pictured together
in the bright spring garden
relaxing
smiling at our two dogs –
look what I once had

8. Pushing Clouds Through the Sky

birds calling
cicadas chirring
surf murmuring,
children's voices far off…
such quietude is golden

green leaves
becoming brown leaves
become nothing…
what is the point of life
lingering in brittle brown

empty road
edged by winter-bare trees –
verdant spring
will bring new life again
though not for all of us

burying his ashes
beneath a eucalypt
to join the dust
of our daughter's life,
just as he'd requested

rooftop terrace
palm trees pushing clouds
through the sky
white doves in the sunset
white sails on the sea

a collaborative tanka string written by *Amelia* with Margaret Chula in the Portland Japanese Garden on 1 September 2015, and published in *Ribbons*, Fall 2015, edited by David Rice

Reflections

morning coolness
dewdrops on the needles
of coastal pines
my sandals leave wet footprints
on old cobblestones

arm-branches
lifting to the light sky
leaves blend gently
green on green on green –
summer woodland garden

in the lower pond
pods of golden koi
flock for food
glint of coins
embedded in mud

the waterfall tumbles
noisy and white,
reflections
of a stone lantern waver
beneath bright patterns

bamboo deer-scarer
fills with water – then
clunks down on the rock
a baby vole crawls
across the pathway

memories
of my children skipping
along narrow lanes
between Kyoto temples
in our other life

two collaborative tanka strings written by Amelia with Jan
Foster, published in *Ribbons*, 2016, edited by David Rice
(Amelia's tanka are in italics in 1; Jan's in 2)

1. Lost Innocence

raucous cackle
of kookaburras
shatters
the pre-dawn peace
– the truce between us over

early mornings
shared just with birds, dogs
and my thoughts
blissful – until he
brings forth his half-empty cup

across the fields
mist settles in hollows
drifting…
your once sharp mind
now veiled in confusion

on the way
we view clear-cut mountains
bright blue lakes…
blizzards white-out most things
from the downhill journey

shielded
by the cloak of routine
I manage
to keep moving on
through this storm of grief

2. Survivors

morning after
serene morning, birds sing
all around
this tapestry life
of love, longing, and loss

his easy grin
charms my granddaughter
both survivors
in this patchwork world
of disability

post polio
I couldn't turn cartwheels
though my heart
performed acrobatics –
now I know whom to love

mesmerised
by two hawks' aerial dance,
I'm saddened
we humans suffer
such earthbound limitations

forever
feeling freer in water
than on land,
I breaststroke across the bay
buoyed by a rising tide

on this clear night
a silver moon-bridge beckons
beyond the shore
what possibilities –
my feet on a new path

a tanka tale published in *Ribbons* tanka prose section 2016, edited by Autumn Noelle Hall

1. Still Perfect

a voice I love
sings from across the sea
'come soon
the blossoms are starting
Grandma, come soon'

So I fly over the Pacific Ocean to Seattle, arriving late at night in the wake of a wind-storm.

Next morning, nine-year-old Stephen and I set off for his school.

As we walk up the hilly street lined with deep pink, double-petalled cherry blossom trees, he mourns 'They were much prettier yesterday, before the storm.'

Then he stoops, picks up a fallen flower and hands it to me. 'This one's still perfect, though.'

precious, precious
such moments, such memories –
if only
my mind can keep its clear recall
old age may not be so bad

my contribution to Journeys into Tanka, a special feature in *Ribbons*, spring/summer 2016

My tanka journey began a very long time ago: it was at the Australian National University in Canberra in 1962, while studying Japanese classical literature, that I first encountered, through *The Tale of Genji*, this amazing poetic form. Fast forward thirty-six years and I became involved in translating modern and contemporary Japanese tanka in order to share their splendour with English readers. This in turn led to a strong interest in writing my own tanka. In 2016 I continue happily translating and composing tanka.

> *here I am*
> *all these years later*
> *still tanka-ing*
> *in my sunny homeland*
> *still loving light and learning*

within *Ribbons: Tanka Society of America Journal*, there is a section called The Tanka Café, edited by Michael McClintock. For each issue of *Ribbons*, Michael suggests a theme on which to submit a single tanka for his Tanka Café. Here are the theme tanka which I had published in the Tanka Café, late 2010 to 2018

Things That Fly

    through wide windows
    a patternless swirling
    of seagulls
    in the blue and white sky –
    no end to this longing

~~~~

Solitude and Loneliness

    'I want to die
    before the next winter'
    she confides
    as we walk our dogs
    'I've outlived all my friends'

Wandering

    dwarf maple
    all of its limbs greened
    with soft moss –
    and when the rolling stone
    has finally settled?

Changing Your Mind

>coldest summer
>for fifty years, they say –
>you betrayed me,
>never again will I try
>to make new friendships

Horizon

>thunder booming
>a rooster crowing
>valiantly
>she faces a weekend
>of whatever…

Autumn Locales

>garden party:
>from beyond gold-leafed trees
>in madonna blue skies
>cathedral bells ring out
>this autumn afternoon

A Change in the Weather

>the wind changed
>and Mary Poppins
>disappeared –
>where have they all gone,
>my lost loved ones

Historical Events*

    both sons
    drowned in the tsunami…
    too quiet
    at home now, he says
    in a whisper

The Afterlife

    nightly
    I dream into life
    those who
    surely can have
    no other existence

Colours

    clifftop park:
    winter wattle's yellow blooms,
    a hawk draughting
    between ultramarine
    and azure – I'm here, now

Heirlooms/Relics

    this relic
    of crueler times, treasured
    by my mother
    her mink stole now tumbled
    among the grandkids' costumes

---

* This was selected as Members' Choice Tanka from the Tanka Café by poet Edward J. Reilly and published again in *Ribbons*, Spring/Summer 2013.

Birds

    Christmas morning:
    not flights of angels
    but cockatoos
    in wing-beating white clouds
    flow over our valley

The End

    'the fifth line
    is the most important,
    tanka should
    build and build,' I repeat
    at yet another workshop

The Shadows of Things

    Shadow
    my aunt named her black poodle,
    and he was…
    together they lived
    together they died

You and the Natural World

    wisteria
    blooms purple in the park
    each spring
    I don't see you, somehow
    I fail to flower

Response to a Novel*

> The Translator:
> how much like Hanne's story
> might mine have been
> had I chosen to stay
> with that Japanese lover

Simple Pleasures

> morning shadows
> across the rough sports ground
> a small white dog
> chases balls, bounding and leaping
> behind my sleepless eyes

Poems of Spring and Summer

> from the east
> comes a strong summer sun
> on Christmas Day
> in the Tasman Sea
> all is calm, all is bright

Self-discovery

> waiting
> for him to stop breathing
> waiting
> to start a new life
> that I do not want

---

* *The Translator* by Nina Schuyler

tanka published in *Ripples in the Sand*, the Tanka Society of America anthology, 2016, edited by Jenny Ward Angyal and Susan Constable

there's a blonde girl
running with her black dog
through the fields
of my days, of my dreams,
forever in summertime

~ ~ ~ ~ ~

blue gentians
an intensity of colour
cascading
over the rockery –
no light now in his old eyes

~ ~ ~ ~ ~

Tanka published in themed *Season's Greetings Letter* (SGL) edited by Mohammed H. Siddiqui. These have appeared previously in my earlier collections.

2005: Rainbow

    in the rain
    at the traffic lights
    a young woman
    struggling with her child,
    back to the rainbow

2006: Mist/Fog

    a deer cries
    in the misted park
    splinters of ice
    slide over the pond
    and into my heart

    mist flattened
    grey-green hills ride along
    with the train
    travelling from home
    travelling for love

2007: Pond

    small birds skim
    a Monet-like pond
    dabbed pink
    with water lilies in bloom –
    I open my laptop

2010: Dawn/Sunrise

          a warm night
          lightens into morning –
          I can see
          the shapes of things, just
          not what to do with my life

          ~ ~ ~ ~

          palm tree dawn
          over Waikiki…
          rising early
          to watch the sea change
          from silver to turquoise

          ~ ~ ~ ~

          this dawn sun
          a luminous orange disk
          balanced on cloud
          over unpredictable surf
          and my plans for the day

          ~ ~ ~ ~

          two pelicans
          stand on the sunrise sand,
          a fishing boat
          zips up the channel –
          all this, just for me

2011: Dusk/Sunset/Twilight

                      incomplete moon
                      floating over gold streaks
                      of sunset clouds…
                      we stay on the balcony
                      looking forward together

2012: Trees/Forest/Jungle

                      pear trees in bloom
                      and from the spring earth
                      flare tulips
                      lighting a path
                      from March to April

                            ~ ~ ~ ~

                    a deer steps
                    from the enchanted forest
                    with two fawns
                    frisking close behind…
                    tremble of summer leaves

2013: Shadows

> sunshine, shadows
> my life, my poetry…
> I drive past
> a gaggle of bright cyclists
> swooping out from the forest

2014: Wind/Breeze

> did summer leaves
> cluster so tightly
> when they were new?
> is there comfort in closeness
> before cool breezes blow

> words scattered
> by the autumn wind
> colouring
> my poems in shades
> of scarlet and gold

2015: Silence

> your silence
> seems impenetrable –
> this time
> I won't be seduced
> into speaking first

2016: Stillness

> one still dove
> on the tv antenna
> at six o'clock –
> like me, an early riser
> or escaped from somewhere
>
> a white heron
> stands on its reflection
> in the mirror lake
> the stillness so needed
> for my shifting heart
>
> autumn afternoon
> a stillness of white clouds
> in azure bright
> I empty my mind, fill it
> with chrysanthemums
>
> Basho's frog
> his pond swim over,
> sits in the stillness
> of the perfumed heart
> of a dappled camellia

2017: Loneliness
Lonely

        around the pond
        ferns touching their reflection –
        how lonely
        you say you are when I leave
        even for the shortest while

        is melancholy
        really more interesting
        than contentment?
        so many tanka sing
        songs of loneliness

a collaborative string with *Genie Nakano* published in her book *Storyteller*, 2014

Everything Is Not Enough

resentful
at being woken
so early
my mood swings around
with flocks of rosy clouds

your coffee kiss
brings me to the place
I want to be –
stepping into this day
fragrant with carnations

wedding bouquet
of pale pink carnations
silver ribbons
trailing such youthful hopes
and now…

your hair has greyed
yet the fire of our love
still burns –
come closer and you'll see
its reflection in my eyes

on the surface
of an old garden pond
light refracted
following the ripples
koi mouths gulp for food

my loved ones
are always hungry
everything
is not enough
I want to give more

once a week
for thirty brief minutes
our voices join
while the ocean between us
is rolled away

waves across the world
static on the lines –
longing
for the moment
when we can touch again

individual tanka published in *Take Five: Best Contemporary Tanka*, vol. 3, 2011, and vol. 4, 2012, edited by M. Kei

> slipping on rocks
> the child grasps my hand
> suddenly
> I'm determined to live
> to a great old age

~~~~

> lines of ducks
> criss-crossing the lake
> constantly
> changing formation
> like most extended families

~~~~

> the corsages
> that man always brought her
> cream gardenias
> how I hated the scent
> of her betrayals

~~~~

she leaned there
against the persimmon tree
waving goodbye –
neither of us said
see you next time

~ ~ ~

capricious spring
dark clouds and scudding wings
just when
the flowers and I
felt ready to bloom*

~ ~ ~

from Europe
your daytime calling
my deep night,
our voices making love
along the seabed**

* 'capricious spring' was previously published in the New Zealand journal *Kokako*, number 14.
** 'from Europe' has also been published in *100 Tanka by 100 Poets of Australia & New Zealand*, 2013, edited by Amelia Fielden, Beverley George & Patricia Prime.

Individual tanka published in *The Right Touch of Sun*, Tanka Society of America anthology, 2017, edited by David Terelinck

>   months later
>   still shaking from the mat
>   soft ginger hairs
>   all that remains of the dog
>   guaranteed not to shed

~~~~

>   bare limbs
>   now clad in green leaves –
>   I glanced away
>   and the children moved on
>   into their distant lives

~~~~

>   smoky dusk
>   winter's darkness closing
>   a short day
>   of busyness, before
>   the long loneliness

Is Love Enough

is love enough…
what does one need to be
a good spouse
surfing the peaks and troughs
as the years roll on

long hot summer
haunted by the demon
dementia –
husband beyond rescue
I must rescue myself

turning my face
towards the blue horizon,
I pause
on the shore of the hospice
to swallow my emotions

'it's over' –
sorrow swells in the room,
an ocean
sucking me down, dumping me
on the sands of loneliness

Wild Voices: An Anthology of Small Poems & Art by Women, 2016, edited by Caroline Skanne

>   mid-argument
>   I look out of the window
>   remark on
>   a Bird of Paradise
>   flamboyantly in flower

>   ~~~~

>   no microphone
>   the political speakers
>   outperformed
>   by a magpie chorus
>   perched above the dais

Previously Unpublished Work

Solo Tanka Strings

1. Around a Chinese Garden – In Portland, Oregon

water lilies
some in bud, some full bloom
some decaying
in nature as in life
Lan Su Chinese garden

tortured
into a single thin trunk
three gingkos
thrust miniature leaves
towards white sunshine

crossing
a courtyard floored with pebbles
in the pattern
of 'plum blossoms on cracked ice'
we tread the scholars' way

Year of the Horse:
tiny model colts
stranded
on a moss island
in a pan jing pot

pink lotus
rising high from the pond
where a stone ship
is anchored by a willow –
water falling over rocks

four square lanterns
in the Hall of Brocade clouds
lighting dreams
of tranquillity
with goldfish and peonies

green tea mooncakes
sweet winter melon juice
to the wailing
from a Chinese zither
the calligrapher rests

below the tea-house
an empty wooden boat drifts
across its reflection
crooked concrete bridges, hot
on this summer afternoon

2. Skating Rinks

over there
autumn means Halloween
then Thanksgiving,
while here we're straggling
blandly into summer

over there now
school-free days are cool days,
no snow yet
the kids' fun turns wintry,
skating rinks reopen

from over there
family pictures reach us
on Facebook
the tween in turquoise tights
stands smiling by the ice

over there
the younger brother's a blur
of speed-skating
and I thank the time lapse
for my absence of concern

over there
the photographer,
my daughter, still
remembers rink lessons
of thirty years ago

and here I
recall her excitement
buying white boots
with hard-earned dollars
from after-school jobs

the vast ocean
between these Ice Lands
is bridged
by dreams frosted with age
etched in figure eights

3. Seattle Respite
April 2016

heading north
my train passes Boeing Field
in the sunset
anticipation flares –
six months since I've seen the kids

arrived again
into a spring of fresh leaves
I am greeted
by my granddaughter's new height,
my grandson's great grin

apple blossoms
blurring the morning view
from my window
I hear only silence – then
an excitement of crows

parkland meadows
of dandelions and daisies
round the lake
brown duck wings flapping,
April mists rising

white tulips
cluster near their front porch
nothing
and everything here
is a part of me

vased tulips
colours unmatched, spilling spring
on the mantle
the clutter of family life
so welcome, so welcome

deep pink
double cherry blossoms
presented
in a giant's bouquet
to the pale blue sky

front gardens
blooming with bluebells
like forest floors
beside the bus lane…
spring in suburbia

walking home
from piano lessons
past daffodils
under the cherry blossoms,
I am old, the year is young

her robust kids
playing near fragile blooms,
my daughter
still researching a cure
for childhood leukaemia

intense
in colour, tenacious
in flower
blue gentians cascading
over the rockeries

waking early
with an insistence of doves
and rose scents
through my opened window
I see a better future

a dogwood tree
in gorgeous pink bloom
on the dog walk
dispelling my bad dreams
along with night's darkness

the fragrance
from white lilac subtler
than expected –
letting go of the old age
I had imagined for us

white tulips
white rhododendrons
such contrasts
with the scarlets and crimsons –
life as a kaleidoscope

pink snow
on cherry blossom road
a black Lotus
parked beneath the trees
becomes a Disney car

thirteen days:
all their blossoms fallen
the cherry trees
are filled with summer leaves
and my stay is half over

at the Seattle Japanese Gardens

        azaleas
        azaleas, azaleas
        everywhere
        all shapes, all colours –
        May is coming

        chasing a carp,
        the hyperactive
        mandarin drake –
        my planning as perilous
        as the Cascade ranges

        reflected
        in muddied waters
        iris blades
        wavering like these thoughts
        of a wintry future

4. Forget-Me-Nots and the House of Music
July/August 2016

bright flowers bloom
through the subtle summer
in Seattle
I live a younger life,
old ways left across the sea

early mornings
with jet planes crashing the clouds,
Canada geese
honking their V flight paths,
I nest in a comfort zone

sweet fragrance
from daphne at the front gate
borders
the chaos of these kids
and their music-making

flown away
from winter's dark days
I can stroll
streets of daisies and roses,
swim in a lake's cool waters

white dahlias –
in childhood memories
Dad grew them
all in velvet colours
crimson, orange and gold

encountered
on my morning walk circuit,
both backlit:
a large white retriever
and a Chinese parasol

my daughter
is guiding her daughter
through teendom
much as I did, back then –
lavender, more lavender

a blue sail
blown across the blue lake
under blue sky –
whoever designated blue
the colour of depression

sculls sliding
in and out of lake mists –
I wonder
whether my explanation
is clear enough for her

the dull sky
of Seattle this morning
grows more brilliant
afternoon into evening –
unlike my life's progress

around Green Lake
my grandkids paddle kayaks
in the sunshine
I sit watching with pride,
totally relaxed…for now

in the night sky
I see a star flying fast
to somewhere –
how long can I go on
crossing the world for love

5. Sweet & Sour

Friday nights
in Sydney's Chinatown
the restaurant
above a strange-smelling shop
cluttered with foreign stuff

no tablecloths
on round laminex tables
course after course
of savoury dishes
steaming, glistening

boiled white rice
in hand-sized bowls
with chopsticks
I used more skilfully
than knife fork and spoon

jasmine tea
from little willow-patterned cups
without handles
without milk or sugar –
different customs here

my parents
their cousins and friends
smoked Craven As –
finding them ashtrays,
inhaling grey puffs of smoke

an only child
on those fragrant evenings,
a lucky child
in the post-war forties' life
of my loved small Sydney world

Responsive Tanka Strings

(i) written with *Kath Abela Wilson* (USA)

Finding the Way

at Mt Fuji
half a century ago
I believed
in love lasting forever –
how young, how naïve I was

bobbing
on the South China Sea
a hat –
together we knew
we'd find a way

streets with no names
non-sequential numbers,
a strange city –
he sent me a map, but
I never made it to his home

waves of my mind
go up and down my legs…
the thrill
of knowing I am here,
in Tokyo

separated
by the Pacific Ocean
from my homeland,
an exotic culture
turns me into a poet

(ii) written with *Owen Bullock* (New Zealand)

Stepping Lightly

black swans
stepping lightly
into the sky –
whatever you believe
seems to be true

heaven's music
tonight in the vastness
Tennyson's
'tintinnabulation
of the everlasting stars'

a thrush
calls out the dream
from the air
I was here
I was here before

dreamless nights
follow the drifting through
dreamlike days –
where do possums hide
from the fierce summer sun

she calls him
and he calls her…
her other self
and his conscience
fly into the earth

Tanka Tales

1. All Grown-Up

When their beloved Cairn terrier died, Mum and Dad divorced.

By that time I had been living out of town in a university college for over a year.

Legally I was an adult.

Emotionally I was, my parents considered, capable of maintaining a separate relationship with each of them.

True enough…but suddenly I had three addresses, and no home.

> *home is*
> *where the heart is,*
> *so 'they' say…*
> *and if there is no home*
> *is there no heart?*

2. Aimez-Vous Brahms*

Mid-morning on my sixtieth birthday: several congratulatory phone calls already received, a delivery of champagne and flowers comes from my godmother.

You go to our bedroom, return holding an unwrapped pack of Frank Sinatra CDs, with a discount sticker on it. Hand it to me, and say 'Happy Birthday'.

I have never liked Frank Sinatra. Leaving your gift on a pile of disks, I walk out of the house with our dogs.

'Aimez-vous Brahms?*
I know that you won't
have read the book,
but did you never
see the movie…

---

* *Aimez-vous Brahms* (*Do You Like Brahms*) is a novel by the French author Françoise Sagan, in which the middle-aged heroine's long-time lover shows no awareness of her tastes, for example in music. A younger man, eager to please, comes onto the scene… In 1961, this story was made into a film starring Ingrid Bergman and Anthony Perkins, with the title *Goodbye Again*.

3. Not Daily Life

A day of peaceful stimulation in an airy room by a lagoon.

Nothing jarring in these background sounds:

> a small aircraft, passing in the distance
> the soft swish of the overhead fan
> intermittent chirping from birds all around

Here I can be my contemplative, poetry-focused self.

Is this the 'real' me? If it is, how infrequently do I relax into this self.

Rather than resent the way daily life forces me to spend much of my time in other modes, I should try to be truly present on this occasion, and hope its effects will linger long.

> *what are they*
> *escaping from, to come here?*
> *I share space*
> *in this seminar day*
> *with eighteen other poets*

4. Plus Ça Change

Time for a change

> *another life*
> *responsibility free*
> *calls me*
> *across the ocean*
> *I fly, I fly…*

I change planes in Los Angeles. On the next flight, travelling at a lower altitude, I can look at scenery: the unaltered majesty of snow-covered cones, the silver sheets of water which show the way to Seattle.

The children have been brought to the airport to meet me. I walk towards the luggage carousel. As always they race each other to be the first gathered into my arms.

I open wide my eyes and my heart again: Haylie is beaming a braces' smile; Stephen's new buzz-cut tips my shoulder.

> *nothing changes*
> *except appearances –*
> *love is love*
> *for growing grandkids*
> *for ageing grandmas*

This piece was written in response to a prompt of the word 'change'. There is a French saying: *plus ça change, plus c'est la même chose*, which means 'the more things change, the more they stay the same'.

6. 'Everything is a source of fun...'*

Scene 1, 1956: Canberra High School's biennial Gilbert & Sullivan production.

> *happy actor*
> *soft-voiced singer, I'm chosen*
> *to play*
> *the third maiden, Peep-bo*
> *in an imagined Japan*

Interval   Seven years living and loving in the 'real' Japan

Scene 2, 1978: One evening, as I am about to take a train into Sydney city to see the much-awaited famous visiting D'Oyly Carte company perform, I receive a call from my mother: Grandma has suffered a fatal stroke.

> *D'Oyly Carte*
> *splendidly professional*
> *very funny...*
> *tears stream down my face,*
> *the funeral is next week*

Scene 3, 1981: When Weetangera Primary School stages its brilliantly abridged version, the cast includes my younger daughter.

> *The Mikado*
> *in miniature, fifth graders*
> *costumed mostly*
> *from our family's souvenirs –*
> *'here's a pretty how-de-do'**

Scene 4, 2015: I take Arthur to a delightful pre-Christmas performance by talented members of the Queanbeyan Arts Society, who are accompanied by a full orchestra.

> *'the flowers*
> *that bloom in the spring, tra-la…*
> *hard of hearing*
> *husband misses dialogue*
> *taps out the tunes on his knee*

Finale '…until the shadows fall…'** whenever that is.

> *let's 'sing*
> *a merry madrigal'*
> *for tomorrow*
> *we might die – or*
> *we might not*

* According to Wikipedia, *The Mikado* is one of the most frequently played musical pieces in history. It was first performed in 1885, in London. The composer was Arthur Sullivan, the librettist, W.S. Gilbert. All the asterisked quotations are from Gilbert's lyrics.
** '…until the shadows fall, over one and over all'

Excerpts from Tanka Diaries

1. Most of My Desires

Thursday 16 May 2012 – start of another Japan trip.

In wintry Canberra I board the coach to Sydney; heavy traffic through the peak-hour city.

> looking up
> from the traffic jam
> to ink-blot clouds
> in the twilight sky
> I imagine angels

Friday 17 May – our Jet Star 6 a.m. departure is delayed when a passenger is removed from the aircraft and her luggage has to be offloaded.

> sixty-two years
> I've been flying, still
> that same
> exhilaration
> as the plane rises

Changing planes at Cairns is a pain, but at least Japan is now only seven hours away.

> in my porthole
> clouds piling on clouds –
> somewhere beyond
> are the lofty turrets
> of Osaka Castle

Saturday 18 May – bright warm morning, forecast maximum 26° for Nara.

> breakfasting here
> an ancient pagoda
> within sight,
> I am blissfully
> a long way from home

With Saeko to the downtown shopping arcades, then light lunch with a 'deer parfait' for dessert at a café near the Daigo Temple garden.

> choice no choice –
> were I to live again
> in Japan
> Nara would satisfy
> most of my desires

Afternoon sightseeing in Noriko's car to Isokanai Shrine and Byakugoji Temple.

under a tall camellia bush

> intently
> the caterpillar climbs
> up a thread
> as invisible
> as your support for me

Evening banquet at Kasuga Hotel with eight Japanese poets.

Sunday 19 May – the 'main event': Tanka Concert with piano performances and bilingual tanka readings. Air very humid.

> luminous balls
> of bilingual tanka
> tossed from the stage
> to the audience,
> one Sunday in Nara

Celebratory dinner for twelve was a multi-course, authentically French presentation in his own home by 'Monsieur Nakata', husband of one of Noriko's tanka group members.

Monday 20 May – sightseeing in the morning, tanka workshop in the afternoon.

> canopied
> with the brilliant greens
> of young leaves
> this ancient capital
> serene in early summer

~ ~ ~ ~ ~

> tanka workshop:
> only the seeing-eye dog
> stays silent
> in the creative buzz
> of twenty keen poets

Early evening transfer by train to Kyoto for two nights; weather getting warmer each day.

Tuesday 21 May – hot, hot, hot; morning at the monthly Tōji Temple flea market, then retired to the air-conditioned delights of the Kyoto Station Building and Isetan department store.

Late afternoon, taxi to the Imperial Palace vicinity for meeting with Dr, Nagata, Kawano Yūko's widower, son Jun and daughter Koh, in a private room of a small, classy, traditional Japanese restaurant.

> three years gone
> yet I feel Yūko
> is somewhere
> in this complex city –
> if only I knew where

Invitation to presentation ceremony for Kawano Yūko Poetry Award in November, and discussions of further translation commissions. Then a kaiseki banquet accompanied by much sake.

Wednesday 22 May – alarm clock set for 6.15 a.m. Train in Osaka airport. Flights to Hong Kong via Taipei, and H.K. to Sydney. Coach to Canberra the next day. The 'long way round'!

> the plane lifts
> and already I'm there
> in the land
> of responsibility
> checking my diary

2. 'Festive Season' 2013

Friday 20 December – forecast maximum 37°; spent the morning at Dickson pool keeping cool with Kathleen. Birthday dinner at Iori Japanese restaurant

>seventy-two…
>how has this happened to me
>constantly
>rehearsing my life,
>not ready to be old
>
>family tradition
>of a Christmas tree set up,
>decorated
>on my birthday…that died
>the year we lost our Kerstie*

Saturday 21 December – another hot sunny day; afternoon at the lake, dogs' delight; back home, overhead fan going full bore

>lolling
>on her woolly back
>the white poodle
>seduces the master
>of her new household

---

*Kerstie's birthday was 18 December.

Sunday 22 December – hot; film of *Aida* at the Palace Cinema – terrible!

> a Facebook photo
> of her first solo cake –
> this longing
> for my granddaughter
> to cook in my kitchen

> told of the death
> of yet another ex-spouse
> I ponder
> the nature of attachment,
> not mated for life but…

Monday 23 December – hot; Konni to vet for cortisone shot for chronic itchiness

> Season's Greetings:
> today's card carries
> the message
> from his wife that
> my old lover is dying

> sunshine shimmers
> in the city centre'
> the Salvos' band
> proclaiming 'Silent Night'
> long before the first star

Tuesday 24 December – a little cooler, still no rain

> bone-dry, this field
> where I walk the dogs
> through summer heat –
> a year-end wish, to join
> my family in the snow

Christmas Eve dinner at Gail's apartment with six other adults

>   no kids here
>   too excited to sleep,
>   our pets
>   treat this Eve as just
>   another snoozy night

Wednesday 25 December – cooler, & cloudy; 'only' 26 degrees, opened hamper gift from Seattle; Seattle family phoned us at 10 a.m.; lavish lunch with at the Hyatt with Kathleen & 'pling

>   Christmas morning:
>   not flights of angels
>   but cockatoos
>   in wing-beating white clouds
>   flow over the valley

>   the tinsel
>   always hung heavier
>   on one side,
>   and my neat Grandma
>   never adjusted it

>   long ago
>   my two young daughters
>   polished
>   the silver cutlery
>   for our Christmas table

Thursday 26 December – Australian Boxing Day; Christmas Day in USA; long skype call to the Seattle family, with kids showing us their Santa pressies and so on; lunch at Heather & Peter's – they have air conditioning!

> from Seattle
> apologetically
> my daughter's voice
> 'it was never meant
> to be like this, Mum'

> cherry ripe
> chocolate delight
> sweeter
> than the sweetest
> ripe cherry

3. Blue-sky Days 2014

4 August – relaxing at home in Seattle

>on the lawn
>two black dogs lie listening
>to their girl
>play clarinet tunes
>through the summer dusk

9 August – *Annie* at the Theatre in the Forest on Kitsap Peninsula

>hiking a trail
>in the Kitsap woodlands
>I hear
>the absence of birdsong –
>this is so far from home

12 August – returning from a visit to Alice on Bainbridge Island

>painted on blue sky
>Mt Rainier, soaring
>white-streaked
>a screech of seagulls
>greets our ferry's arrival

16 August – day trip to Crystal Mountain with Marie & Gypsy

>sweet sweet sweet
>the song of three new birds
>flying low
>from pine to pine to pine
>on the mountain top

ski-slope meadows
wild with purple lupins
and white daisies…
at the summit chipmunks
soliciting tourists

17 August – by the Green Lake wading pool

in the lake park
a pied piper blowing bubbles
kids run to catch –
at the curled water's edge
a blue heron, motionless

20 August – on the back deck

lone crow
are you speaking to me?
you're sounding
too pessimistic
for this blue-sky day

21 August – Seattle Rose Garden

time out for me
to smell the garden's roses
as grandchildren
chase around the space
of elderly contentment

22 August – around the suburbs

>   summer's ending
>   a cool wind ruffles the lake,
>   petals fall
>   from hanging flower-baskets,
>   sunshades are folded away

23 August – Whidbey Island 'dog beach'

>   kites in the sky
>   racing dogs on the sand
>   at low tide
>   this steel-blue bay ripples
>   and I breathe slowly

26th August – for Carole

>   once again
>   you are here by Green Lake
>   taking photos
>   of water lilies, once again
>   twelve months have flown by

28 August – off to Portland by Amtrak

>   rosy with dawn
>   on the horizon
>   Mt Rainer –
>   my yellow taxi turns
>   towards the train station

> mile after mile
> of calm pearl-grey water
> on the way
> to the vibrant city
> of my colourful friend

> by the train tracks
> at the edge of a forest
> a small white cross
> heaped about with bright flowers –
> what happened there?

29 August – reading Sonja Arntzen's new scholarly translation of the tenth-century 'Sarashina Diary'

> long ago
> I dipped my toes into
> the waters
> of academia –
> another way not taken

30 August – at University Village

> a humming bird
> stops pedestrian traffic
> hovering
> round petunia pots
> outside the shopping centre

31 August – Stephen

>   the nine-year-old
>   shows me his tidied room,
>   saying 'it's small
>   but big enough
>   for all I own'

1 September – 8202 Ashworth Avenue North

>   a grey squirrel
>   springs up the magnolia
>   in this garden
>   where my grandkids will play
>   for months and months without me

2 September – at Discovery Park

>   where the blue
>   of the Sound, meets the blue
>   of the sky
>   I'll fly away, come back
>   when all is winter-coloured

4. One Week In December

17 December 2014 – This evening finally reached my other home, 8202 Ashworth Avenue North, Seattle. Haylie was wearing the birthday dress I'd sent her this year, to welcome me. And Gypsy greeted me with a border collie 'song'.

> eight years
> of crossing the Pacific
> to be with them…
> what will my grandchildren
> remember from these visits?

18 December – Cloudy but not terribly cold. After the many hours on flights, I was glad to walk Gypsy right around Green Lake.

> winter lake
> morning ducks scissoring
> the silence
> in mottled blue grey brown silk –
> all the joggers wearing gloves

It's dark here at four o'clock. Most of the houses in our street are beautifully decked out with light displays. After school is music practice time: both kids doing piano and clarinet; Haylie has added saxophone and is in her school's jazz band.

> concentrating
> as he plays piano
> Stephen's
> angel face, haloed
> by lights on the Christmas tree

19 December – Showers overnight then fine all day.

    'be careful'
    the porch steps are slippery
    with night rain
    a damaged grandma
    might be a liability

    bird-calls here
    in Seattle just
    seagulls and crows,
    but the children's accents
    ring sweet in my ears

    how white
    the trunks of bare birches –
    winter sun
    flickers uncertainly
    in this snowless city

20 December – My birthday: seventy-three – how did this happen?

    along the street
    gaudy with coloured lights
    crimson maple
    branches strung with raindrops –
    Away in a Manger

21 December – A school skating party for sixth grade students and their families at Seattle Centre. My daughter laces her boots and is first adult on the rink.

> as I watch
> her confident skating
> my mind glides back
> over thirty years
> of our life's surprises

Much later, a well rugged-up family excursion to 'Wildlights' at Woodland Park.

> the night zoo
> is illuminated
> at Christmas time
> away from the brilliance
> meerkats huddled in sleep

22 December – Off to Whistler ski resort in Canada.

> driven slowly
> through an Impressionist's
> blizzard,
> I think of burning soles
> on Sydney's beach sands

23 December on the morning valley trail.

>snow dreaming:
>black dogs prancing and playing
>in a white field
>by Crabapple Creek
>rocks patchworked with crystals

5. Many Homes Or None

Sunday 2 August 2015 – Start of family holiday. Drove north to Anacourtes.

Ferry to San Juan Island; 1¾ hours of beautiful scenery.

> blue silk water
> beneath a white ferry,
> pine islands
> in the distance, painted
> on pale blue sky, snow mountains

Short drive from Friday Harbour to Lakedale Resort and our log cabin.

> log cabin life
> old-fashioned family fun
> for a week
> swimming fishing hiking –
> with of course Wifi

Monday 3 August – Woke to the sound of oars swishing through the lake below our deck.

> bolt upright
> and bonneted, two grannies
> rowing over
> reflected greenery
> in rhythm with the morning

Drove through dense forests to Lime Kiln Lighthouse whale-watching point. For some hours saw no whales, just one large brown seal.

> a blond boy
> watching from the beach
> a harbour seal
> in the kelp, gliding
> and diving – both beautiful

Tuesday 4 August – Morning to Roche harbour. Family went off on bikes for two hours. Gypsy and I relaxed in the local dog park.

> shady meadow
> on top of the steep hill
> just sitting
> with a collie at my feet –
> *where can you live but days**

Around one o'clock we drove further across the island for a picnic lunch.

> along forests
> of giant cedars reaching
> for the bright sky,
> pale purple chicory
> flowers mile after mile

* Philip Larkin

Back at Lakedale a late afternoon of swimming

> my body
> stroking the dark lake,
> two hawks
> skimming the light sky
> …freedom

Wednesday 5 August – Early morning walk with a light cool breeze ruffling the trees.

> a dawn deer
> grazing near our cabin
> gone in a flash –
> this life of appearances
> and disappearances

Thursday 6 August – To American Camp State Park; picnic at South Beach.

> a blonde girl
> running with her black dog
> through the fields
> of my days, of my dreams
> forever in summertime

Friday 7 August – Lovely sunny day. Haylie, Gypsy, and I checked out the shops and picnicked at Friday Harbour while David and Stephen played golf.

        white
        boats and seagulls
        blue
        harbour and sky
        white on blue, white on blue

        a large otter
        or a small harbour seal?
        whichever,
        we're blessed by a clear view
        of its offshore antics

Saturday 8 August – Transferred by ferry to Orcas Island in time for the sunset sea-kayaking tour.

        their kayaks
        slide away, out of sight
        from the beach
        where I wait, sure this time
        they will come back to me

Sunday 9 August – Sharing a 'glamping' tent with Haylie at West Beach.

>   wheatsheaf hair
>   hiding her face, she sleeps,
>   this granddaughter
>   I never thought I'd have
>   such a stake in the future

Monday 10 August – Heard deer on the porch overnight. Stephen caught four fish and a crab before we left West Beach.

>   a boy
>   with his dad, fishing
>   off the pier
>   seagulls circling through blue
>   …this timelessness

Tuesday 11 August – To farm-stay inland on Orcas Island. Idyllic rural setting.

>   in a meadow
>   holding *The Haiku Mind*
>   I breathe in
>   the scent of cypress,
>   breathe out my bad dreams

Wednesday 12 August – Very hilly walk with the kids to Jack's Lake; deep and cool.

> I swim along
> always on the surface
> not daring
> to explore what lies beneath
> this deep lake, this life…

Thursday 13 August – Last day of this trip. Drove into Moran State Park. Hiked there on Mt Constitution before ferrying back to Seattle.

> heading home:
> home is where the heart is,
> so they say –
> for those with divided hearts
> are there many homes or none

6. In the Northern Hemisphere Again

Friday 4 August 2017 in Seattle – Lovely summer weather; walked to kids' morning swim training at Evans Pool

> French lavender
> growing in Seattle
> the grandchildren
> I thought I'd never have –
> scents fade, scents strengthen

Monday 7 August – Lunch outside in the sunshine at Duke's Chowder House with old school friend Ellen, and Stephen.

> meeting once more
> we speak of teachers we shared
> crème brûlées
> some plans for just this year –
> 'the rest is silence'

Wednesday 9 August – Kids practised piano, saxophone, and clarinet in the morning. Afternoon swimming in the lake.

> legacy
> of Grandpa's nimble fingers
> the model plane
> still on the piano top
> waiting for lift-off

Saturday 12 August – Junior triathlon; both kids won their age divisions.

> they stand there
> on the winner's dais
> again –
> will the races to come
> be run as easily

Monday 14 August – Pot luck lunch and Japanese tanka workshop at Fusako Kusumi's splendid house in Bellevue.

> from the garden
> behind that house on the hill
> the long arms
> of a spruce, reaching for clouds –
> too soon I'll fly away

Wednesday 16 August – Poet Carole came from Point Roberts to have a Green Lake stroll and lunch with me.

> lunching
> on the sunlit terrace
> with an old friend
> talking about 'a good death'
> as something quite remote

Friday 18 August – The usual morning music practices.

>'Scenes from Childhood'*
>overlapping love
>for this boy
>for this music – unearned
>the richness of my life

Sunday 20 August – To Carkeek Park on a beautiful morning with all the family, including Gypsy dog.

>a bonded pair
>the girl fourteen years young
>her border collie
>twelve years old, together
>for how much longer

Monday 21st August – Stephen's clarinet audition for the Seattle Youth Symphony Orchestra.

>once again
>the Mozart concerto
>delights me
>in the same measure
>as the young musician

---

* Robert Schumann, Op. 15, No. 1

Tuesday 22 August – Family holiday driving and staying around the Olympic Peninsula to Wednesday 30 August.

Saturday 26 August – Luxurious vacation house in the country.

> twilight at Forks
> an elk in the meadow
> with his herd –
> will anyone care
> to read my diaries

Sunday 27 August – Trail walk and San Duo river picnic in the state park.

> silver birches
> forming a leafy frieze
> by the river
> a father and son fish –
> this final summer month

Monday 28 August – Arrived at Lake Quinault.

> line of sight:
> deep blue lake, white sailboat
> spruce forest
> mountain peaks, unclouded sky
> just this for now

Tuesday 29 August – Full day at Lake Quinault.

> wind music
> high in the spruce forest
> low on the lake…
> first notes of a Mozart
> clarinet concerto

Tuesday 31 August – Back 'home'. Stephen had a cold, so we played board games while Haylie was at cross-country training.

> today, coaching
> this grandson at Scrabble
> I awe him
> with the obscure words
> my dad had at his command

Saturday 2 September – Still hot and very much swimming weather.

> across the pool
> a skein of Canada geese
> glides, honking
> 'our lake again now
> September, September'

Monday 4 September – Kids back to school tomorrow. I leave on Wednesday. Last lake swim.

> Labor Day
> no lifeguards on duty
> at the lake beach
> a few leaves in free fall –
> early spring back home

About the Author

Amelia Fielden was born in Sydney, Australia, 1941. She is an internationally awarded translator and poet.

Qualifications

Bachelor of Asian Studies (Japanese Honours), Australian National University, Canberra

Graduate Diploma of Secondary Education, University of Adelaide, South Australia

Graduate Diploma of Translation (Japanese), University of Canberra

Master of Arts (Japanese Literature), University of Newcastle, New South Wales; Masters' thesis: An Annotated Translation of *My Tanka Diary* by Kawano Yūko

Career

1965–2003, researcher, teacher, translator

Since retiring from full-time work as a senior Japanese translator for the Australian government, Amelia has specialised in translating Japanese literature – primarily, but not exclusively, tanka poetry.

Books translated, or co-translated, by Amelia

(Key: OP – out of print; NLA – available in the National Library of Australia collection)

On Tsukuba Peak: 2000 tanka collection by Kawamura Hatsue; bilingual, Wollongong, NSW, Five Islands Press, 2002 (OP)

Time Passes (Saigetsu): 1995 tanka collection by Kawano Yūko; bilingual; Canberra, ACT, Ginninderra Press, 2002 (OP; NLA)

Vital Forces (Tairyoku): 1998 tanka collection by Kawano Yūko; co-translated with Yuhki Aya; bilingual; Nagoya, Japan, Bookpark, 2004 (OP)

Behind Summer (Natsuno Ushiro): 2003 tanka collection by Kuriki Kyōko co-translated with Yuhki Aya; Canberra, ACT, Ginninderra Press, 2005 (OP; NLA)

As Things Are: 100 tanka selected by Manaka Tomohisa from 10 collections by Kawano Yūko; Canberra, ACT, Ginninderra Press, 2005 (OP; NLA)

On This Same Star ('Will'): 2003 tanka collection by Kitakubo Mariko; bilingual; Tokyo, Japan, Kadokawa Shoten, 2006 (available on amazon.com, at the Pacific Asia Museum, Pasadena, California, through the manager at tailingwong@yahoo.com, and by contacting the poet at tanka@kitakubo.com)

My Tanka Diary (Hizuke no Aru Uta): 2002 prose plus poetry diary by Kawano Yūko; Canberra, ACT, Ginninderra Press, 2006 (OP; NLA)

Ferris Wheel: 101 Modern and Contemporary Japanese Tanka: the work of 56 Japanese poets; co-translated with Uzawa Kozue; bilingual; Boston, USA, Cheng & Tsui, 2006 (available from the publisher www.cheng-tsui.com and on amazon.com) (Awarded the 2007 prize for translation of Japanese Literature by Columbia University, New York, the America Japan Friendship Award, also known as the Donald Keene Award)

Raffaello's Azure: tanka poetry and critical essays by Hazama Ruri; co-translated with the author; bilingual; Tokyo, Japan, Tanka Kenkyusha, 2006 (OP; contact the author at hryamagi@hi3.enjoy.ne.jp)

Cicada Forest: anthology of the work of Kitakubo Mariko; bilingual; Tokyo. Japan; Kadokawa Shoten, 2008 (OP; available on amazon.com or through the poet at tanka@kitakubo.com)

Kaleidoscope: selected tanka of Terayama Shuji; co-translated with Uzawa Kozue; bilingual; Tokyo, Japan, Hokuseidō, 2008 (available from the publisher at www.hokuseido.co.jp or on amazonjapan)

Doorway to the Sky (Sora no Tobira): tanka collection by Tanaka Noriko; co-translated with Ogi Saeko; bilingual; Tokyo, Japan, Tanka Kenkyusha, 2008 (available from the publisher at www.Tanka_Kenkyusha.co.jp)

Aster Flower (Shion): 2009 tanka collection by Kusumi Fusako; bilingual with colour plates; Tenri City, Japan, Tenrijihōsha, 2009 (available from the poet at fkusumi@comcast.net)

The Time of This World: 100 tanka selected by Ōshima Shiyō from 13 collections by Kawano Yūko; Baltimore, Maryland, USA, Modern English Tanka Press, 2010 (OP; a few copies still available from anafielden@gmail.com)

Breast Clouds (Nyubōin):

prize-winning 2008 tanka collection by Tanaka Noriko; co-translated with Ogi Saeko; bilingual; Tokyo, Japan, Tanka Kenkyusha, 2010 (available from the publisher at www.Tanka_Kenkyusha.co.jp)

Snow Crystal Star-shaped: anthology of tanka poetry by Konno Mari; bilingual; Tokyo, Japan, Kadokawa Shoten 2010 (available from the publisher at www.shoten.kadokawa,co,jp)

The Maternal Line (Bōkei): 2008 tanka collection by Kawano Yūko; co-translated with Ogi Saeko; Baltimore, Maryland, USA, Modern English Tanka Press, 2011(OP)

A Bluish White Light: 'a cry from the heart'; tanka about the Fukushima Nuclear Power Plant, by Satō Yūtei; edited by Yasunaga Tatsumi; translated by Amelia Fielden; Matsudo, Japan, JARC Corporation, 2013 (available on amazon.com in paperback or as Amazon 2014 Kindle edition)

Tanka To Eat: themed tanka masterpieces by modern and contemporary Japanese poets, selected and presented with commentaries by Tanaka Noriko; co-translated with Ogi Saeko; bilingual; Port Adelaide, South Australia, Ginninderra Press, 2014 (NLA; available from the publisher www.ginninderrapress.com.au)

From the Middle Country (Naka no Kuni Yori): 2013 collection by Tanaka Noriko; cotranslated with Ogi Saeko; Port Adelaide, South Australia, Ginninderra Press, 2015 (available from the publisher www.ginninderrapress.com.au)

The Journey of My Life: tanka composed by May Yen Ting translated by Amelia Fielden, with commentaries and prose translated by Steven Ting; edited by Ling-Eri Ting and Warren Wu; USA, Prime Paperback, 2014 (available on amazon.com)

Lovely Kimono: themed haiku and tanka by modern and contemporary Japanese poets, selected and presented with commentaries by Tanaka Noriko; co-translated with Ogi Saeko; Port Adelaide, South Australia, Ginninderra Press, 2016 (available from the publisher at www.ginninderrapress.com.au)

For Instance, Sweeheart (Tatoeba Kimi): Forty Years of Love Songs; autobiographical essays and tanka poems written to each other by Kawano Yūko and her husband, Nagata Kazuhiro; first published in

Japanese by Bungei Shunshu Tokyo, in 2011; translated edition, Port Adelaide, South Australia, Ginninderra Press, 2017 (available from the publisher at www.ginninderrapress.com.au)

Original poetry and prose written in English by Amelia Fielden

Eucalypts and Iris Streams: poetry on Australia and Japan in various forms; bilingual; Canberra, ACT, Ginninderra Press, 2002 (OP; NLA; some copies available on amazon.com)

Fountains Play and Time Passes: original tanka in English by Amelia Fielden, together with her translations of selections from 'Time Passes' by Kawano Yūko; bilingual; Canberra, ACT, Ginninderra Press, 2002 (OP; NLA; a few copies still available from anafielden@gmail.com)

Short Songs: individual tanka poems and multi-tanka sequences; bilingual; Charnwood, ACT, Ginninderra Press, 2002 (OP; NLA)

Still Swimming: individual tanka poems plus multi-tanka strings and sequences; Charnwood, ACT, Ginninderra Press, 2005 (OP; NLA)

Baubles, Bangles & Beads: *Threaded Tanka*; Charnwood, ACT, Ginninderra Press, 2007 (OP; NLA; a few copies still available from anafielden@gmail.com)

Light on Water: a collection of individual tanka and tanka strings previously published between 2006 and 2010 in international journals and anthologies; Port Adelaide, South Australia, Ginninderra Press, 2010 (OP; NLA; a few copies still available from anafielden@gmail.com)

Mint Tea From a Copper Pot & Other Tanka Tales: some stories of my life, in poetry and prose, by Amelia Fielden; Port Adelaide, South Australia, Ginninderra Press, 2013 (OP; NLA; a few copies still available from anafielden@gmail.com)

These Purple Years: a collection of individual tanka and tanka strings previously published between 2010 and 2017, in international journals and anthologies; Port Adelaide, South Australia, Ginninderra Press, 2016 (NLA; available from the publisher at www.ginninderrapress.com.au)

Collaborations with other poets

In Two Minds: responsive tanka in themed chapters, written with Australian poet,

Kathy Kituai; Baltimore, Maryland, USA, Modern English Tanka Press, 2008 (OP; a few copies still available from anafielden@gmail.com.au)

Weaver Birds: a bilingual responsive tanka diary written and translated with Japanese-Australian poet, Saeko Ogi; bilingual; Port Adelaide, South Australia, Ginninderra Press, 2010 (NLA; available from the publisher at www.ginninderrapress.com.au)

Yesterday, Today, and Tomorrow: a calendar year of responsive tanka written with Australian poet, Kathy Kituai; Brisbane, Queensland, Interactive Press, 2011 (NLA; available from sales@ipoz.bz and on amazon.com)

Words Flower From One to Another: responsive tanka in themed chapters, written with Japanese-Australian poet, Saeko Ogi; bilingual; Brisbane, Queensland, Interactive Press 2011 (NLA; available from sales@ipoz.bz and on amazon.com)

Conversations in Tanka between Amelia Fielden, Jan Foster, and Friends; several different forms of responsive tanka writing, composed by 23 poets from Australia, France, Japan, New Zealand, South Africa and USA; Port Adelaide, South Australia, Ginninderra Press, 2014 (NLA; available from the publisher at www.ginninderrapress.com.au)

Colouring in: The Four Seasons of Four Poets: Amelia Fielden, Gerry Jacobson, Genie Nakano and Neal Whitman writing, in Australia/American pairs, responsive tanka strings on spring, summer, autumn, and winter; Port Adelaide, South Australia, Ginninderra Press, 2016 (NLA; available from the publisher at www.ginninderrapress.com.au)

Tanka anthologies and collections edited or co-edited by Amelia Fielden

Food For Thought: an anthology of new tanka on a theme, written by 45 Australian poets, collected and edited by Amelia Fielden; Port Adelaide, South Australia, Ginninderra Press, 2011 (NLA; available from the publisher at www.ginninderrapress.com.au)

The Melody Lingers On: an anthology of tanka on musical themes written by 55 Australian poets; collected and edited by Amelia Fielden; Port Adelaide, South Australia, Ginninderra

Press, 2012 (NLA; available from the publisher at www.ginninderrapress.com.au)

Music of the Heart: Australian and Japanese tanka on musical themes, selected by Amelia Fielden and Noriko Tanaka; edited and translated by Amelia Fielden and Saeko Ogi; bilingual; Port Adelaide, South Australia, Ginninderra Press, 2014 (NLA; available from the publisher at www.ginninderrapress.com.au)

100 Tanka by 100 Poets of Australia and New Zealand – one poem each; selected and edited by Amelia Fielden, Beverley George & Patricia Prime; Port Adelaide, South Australia, Ginninderra Press, 2013 (NLA; available from the publisher at www.ginninderrapress.com.au)

Storyteller: individual tanka, tanka sequences (some written responsively with other poets) and tanka prose by Genie Nakano, edited by Amelia Fielden and Ellen Weston; California, USA, Purple Aura Press, 2014 (available from the poet at genieyogini@gmail.com, and on amazon.com)

All You Need Is Love: the theme of 'love', interpreted widely by over 60 Australian poets; Port Adelaide, South Australia, Ginninderra Press, 2015 (available from the publisher at www.ginninderrapress.com.au and on amazon.com)

Poems to Wear: a Japan/Australia production; Part I: Japanese tanka selected, with commentaries added, by Noriko Tanaka and translated by Amelia Fielden and Saeko Ogi; Part II Australian tanka collected and edited by Amelia Fielden; Port Adelaide, South Australia, Ginninderra Press, 2016 (available from the publisher at www.ginninderrapress.com.au)

Poetry-related activities

Member of the Japan Tanka Poets' Society and its Tanka Journal since 1999

Member of the Tanka Society of America since 2000

Member of the Tanka Society of Canada since 2005

Foundation member of the Limestone Tanka Poets, Canberra, Australia

English tanka published regularly in journals worldwide – for example in *Eucalypt* and *paper wasp* (Australia), *Gusts* (Canada), the *Tanka Journal* (Japan), *Kokako* (New Zealand), *Presence* and *Skylark* (UK), *Atlas Poetica*, *red lights*, *Ribbons*, *Moon-bathing* (USA), *100 Gourds* and *cattails* (on line), and in a number of international anthologies from 2001 onwards

Presenter of translation seminars and tanka workshops in Australia, Japan, and USA

Participated in International Tanka Conventions in 2000 (Vancouver), 2006 (Honolulu), 2009 (Tokyo). In 2009 was one of the judges of the associated English tanka competition

Appeared on NHK *Tanka Forum* television program with Kawano Yūko in 2000 and 2005

A special guest at the Imperial Palace, Tokyo for the Annual Imperial New Year Tanka Poetry Gathering in January 2008

Interests

Japan, swimming, reading, attending ballet and opera performances, having fun with grandchildren and pets

www.ingramcontent.com/pod-product-compliance
Lightning Source LLC
Chambersburg PA
CBHW071804080526
44589CB00012B/685